BIG CAT STUDIO

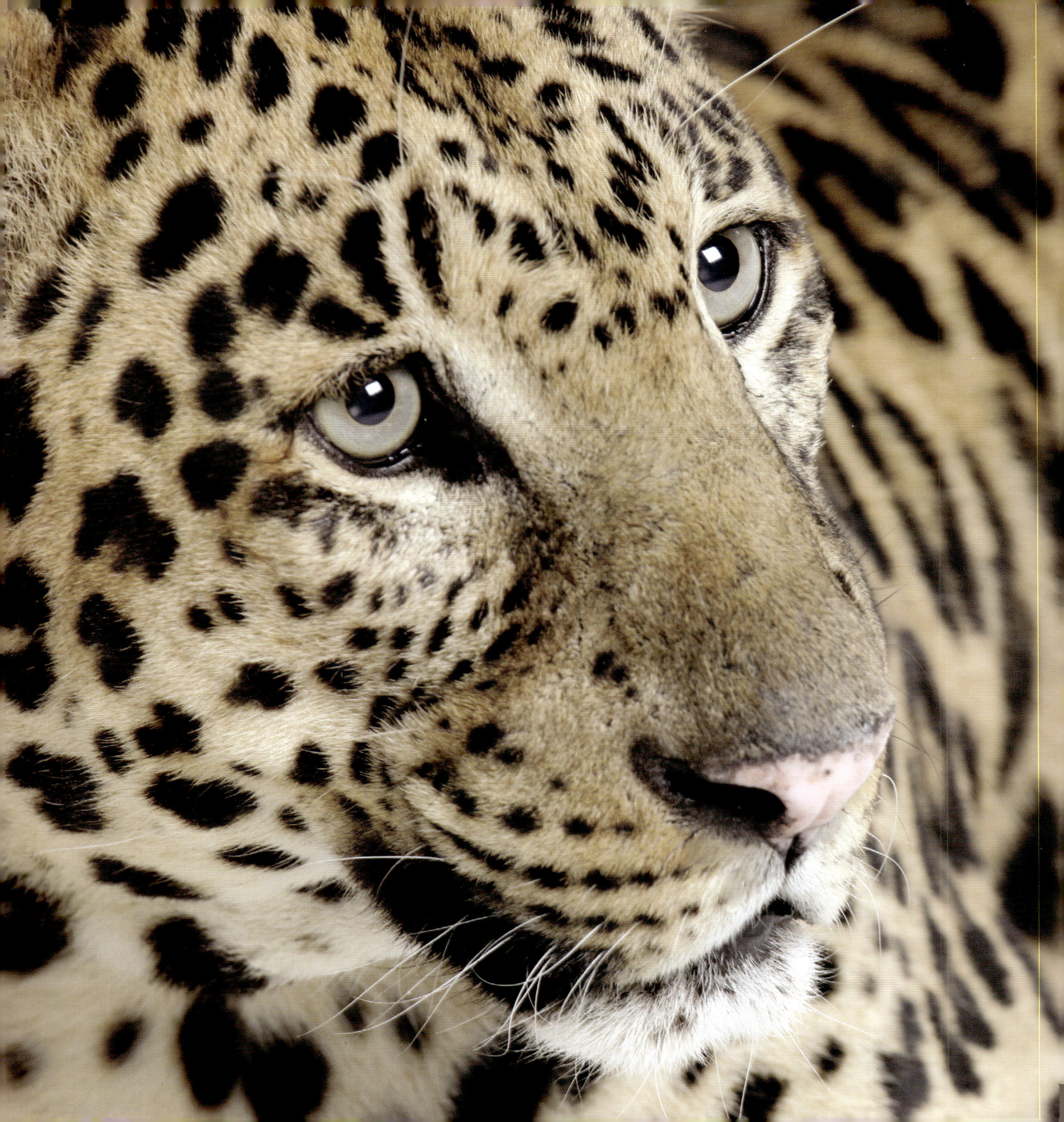

BIG CAT STUDIO

DR BHAGAVAN ANTLE
Photography by **Barry Bland**

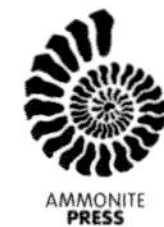

First published 2009 by
Ammonite Press
An imprint of AE Publications Ltd
166 High Street, Lewes, East Sussex BN7 1XU

ISBN 978-1-906672-66-9

A catalogue record for this book is available from the British Library.

Photographer: Barry Bland
Picture Editor: Ben Churcher
Editor: Virginia Brehaut
Design: Ginny Zeal

Colour origination by GMC Reprographics
Printed and bound by Hung Hing Co. Ltd. in China

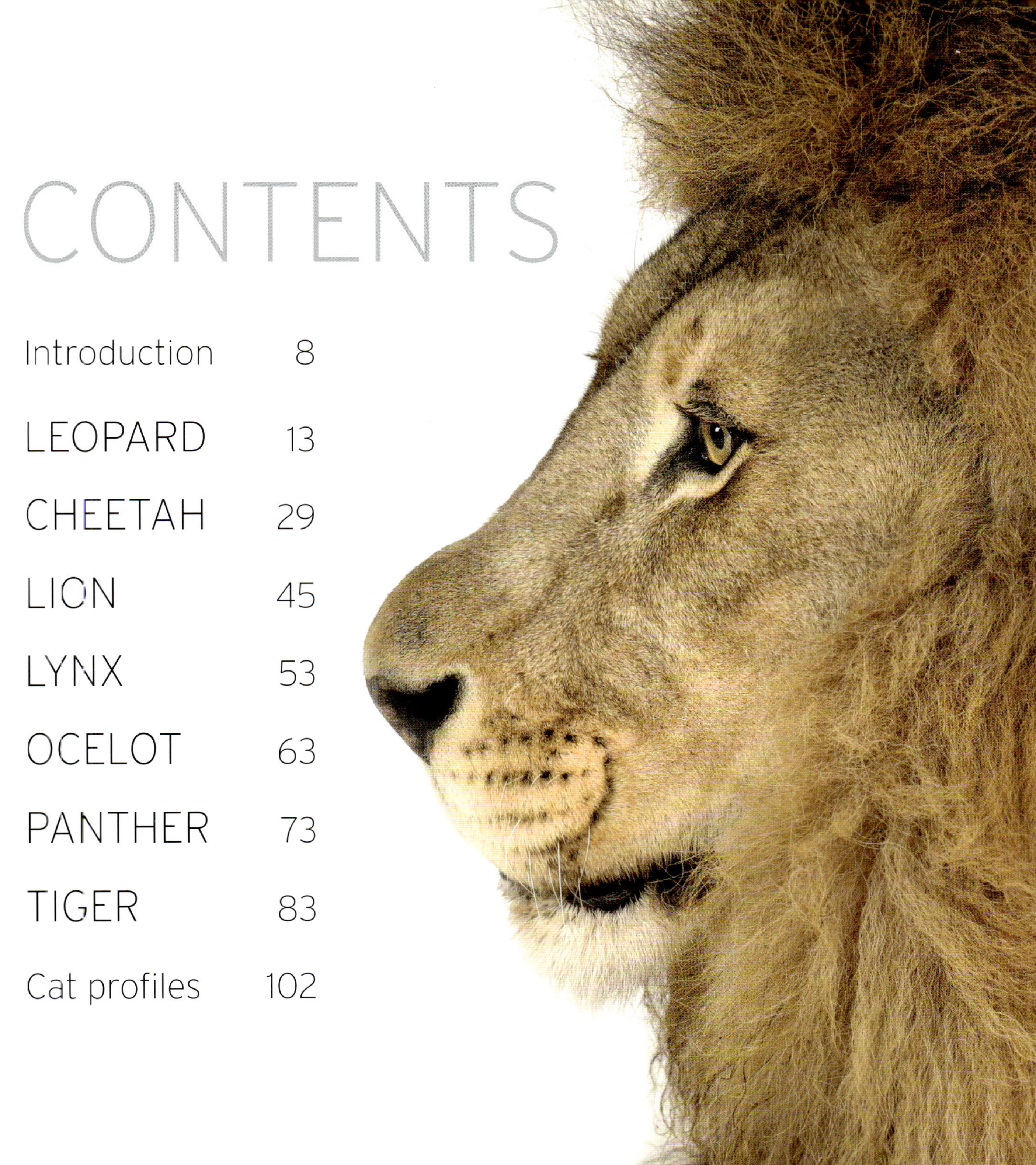

CONTENTS

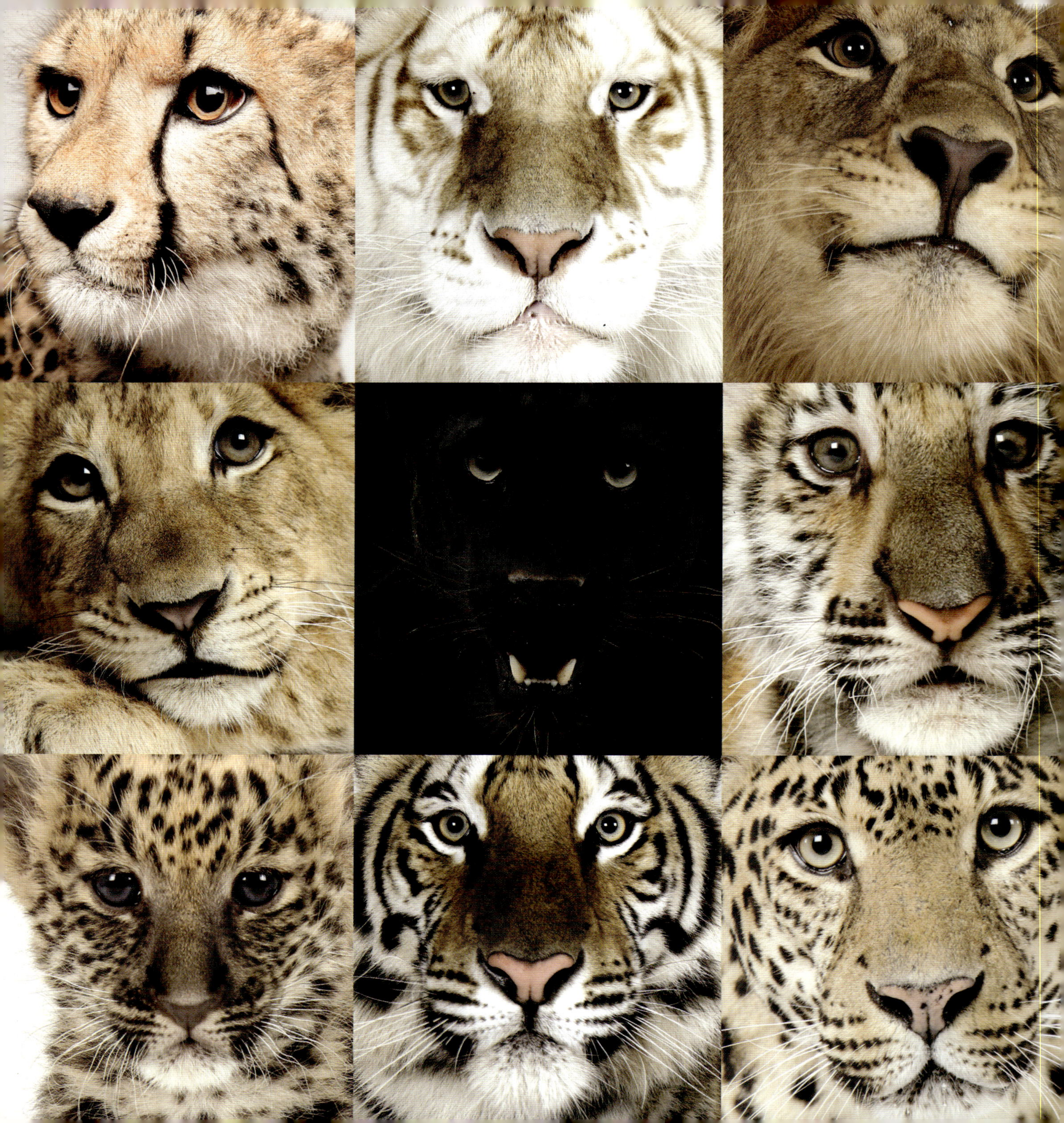

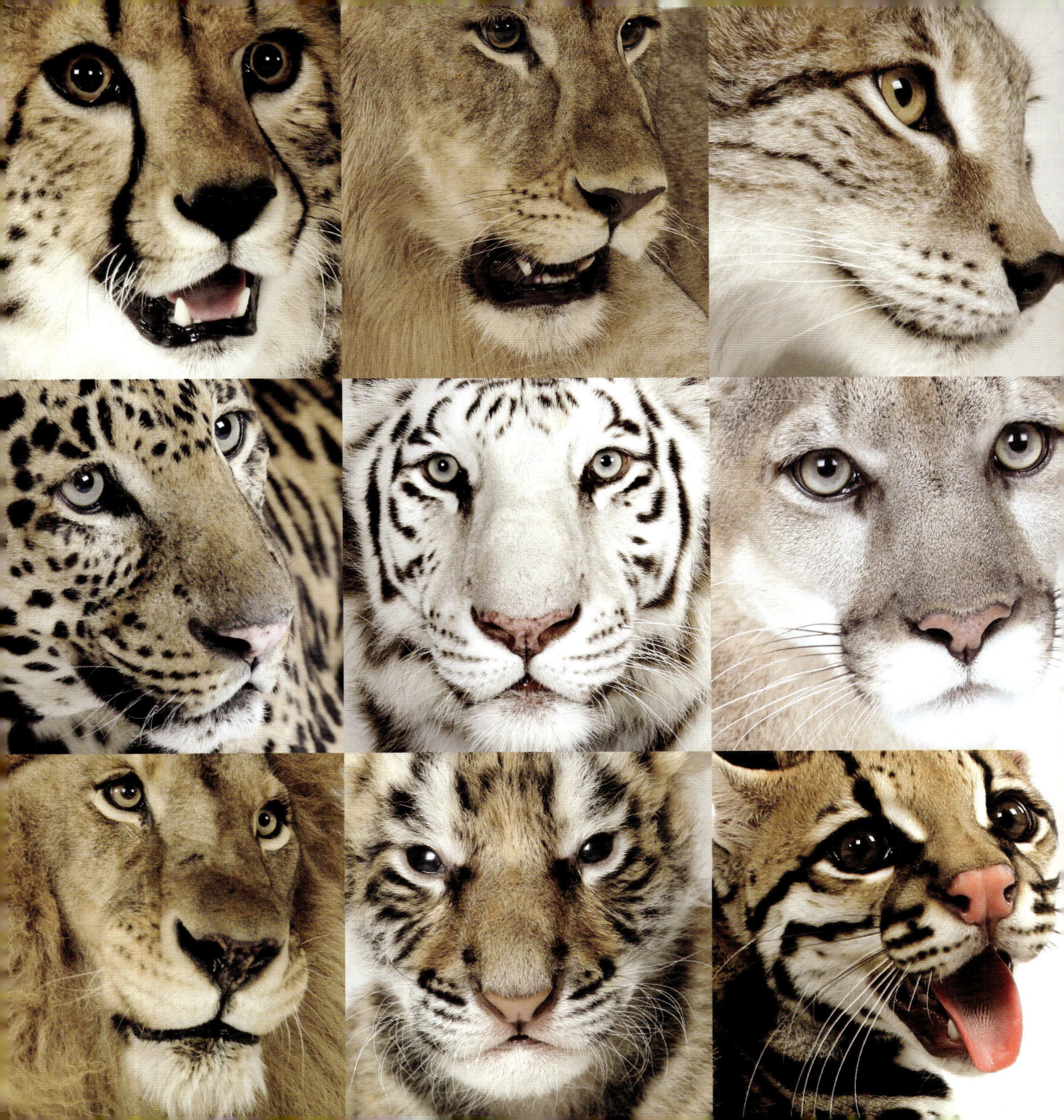

INTRODUCTION

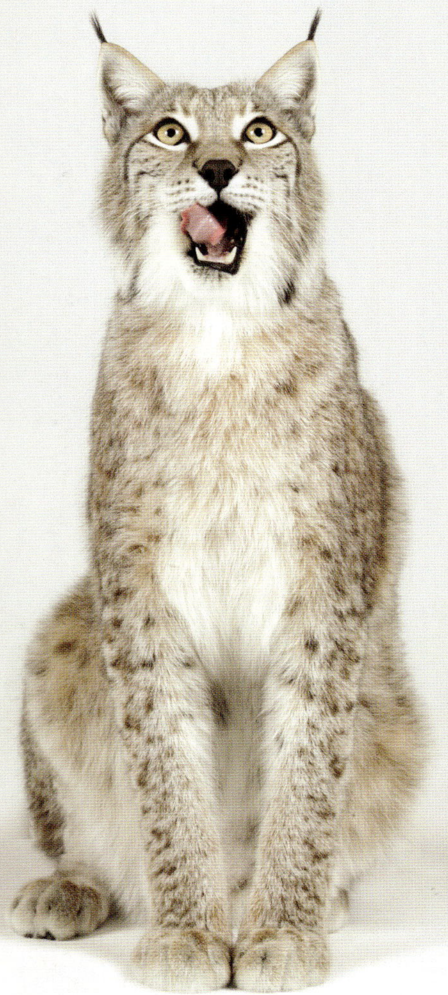

Morning illuminates a dense jungle. Herons and peacocks emerge out of the shadows and shake off the night. A gossamer mist rises from rivers and ponds. Suddenly from the distance comes a rumble. The sound is deep and resonant, like an earthquake threatening to burst through the ground. Water buffalo and sambar deer raise their heads and stare in the direction of the sound. Then silence. A five-hundred-pound Bengal tiger – nature's last sentinel – has moved on.

Memorable encounters such as this have occurred many times on my journeys through India and Africa and they have inspired me for more than twenty-five years. Tigers and other big cats command our attention. Their beauty, power and grace are unrivalled. Being in the physical presence of such a big cat can be life transforming. This book was created for two reasons: to provide you with a taste of that life-transforming experience and to invite you to meet these magnificent creatures yourself as our guest at the T.I.G.E.R.S. (The Institute for Greatly Endangered and Rare Species) Preserve in Myrtle Beach, South Carolina, USA.

Originally I was trained as a physician but it took only a few months of working with tigers and other endangered species to discover that people responded more to an encounter with a big cat than to anything I could have told them as a doctor. To gaze into the eyes of a big cat is to look into the depths of our own souls. We have an existential connection to these wondrous creations of nature. Our fate is tied to theirs, and my life's mission is to convey that message to as many people as possible.

In the 1980s I created a travelling show that provided audiences with just such a face-to-face encounter with rare species. The message of the travelling show was simple: these magnificent creatures are facing extinction. They need our help. We humans have infringed on the natural world, and here are the beautiful animals whose very existence we are threatening. The results were spectacular. Everyone wanted us to bring the animals to their event, and over the next few years my staff and I mounted hundreds of shows featuring tigers, panthers, leopards, and other rare creatures. Word reached Hollywood and we were called to provide animals for movies such as *Ace Ventura*, *Jungle Book*, *Doctor Dolittle*, *Mighty Joe Young* and for commercials for MGM, Exxon, and a host of other high-paying accounts.

T.I.G.E.R.S. PRESERVE

With the proceeds from these assignments we purchased land in Myrtle Beach, South Carolina, as a home for our animal family. Over the years we added to the property and built habitats that replicated the wide-open spaces these wonderful creatures knew in the wild. Twenty-five years after it first began, T.I.G.E.R.S. is now home to more than 100 endangered big cats and other animals. The preserve covers 50 acres (20ha) and includes a jungle garden, a forest lagoon, a glass swimming pool for elephants and tigers, and an open-air veranda overlooking a raceway where pumas, cheetahs and other big cats reach speeds of 55mph (88kph) or more.

Touring the T.I.G.E.R.S. Preserve is unlike any other experience on earth, an experience that is represented in the images you see here. Visitors cradle baby tigers in their laps. Guests take turns stroking the leathery hide of a majestic African elephant. They exchange affectionate hugs with orangutans. They meet rare birds of prey. Time and again we have seen people walk away from these experiences transformed. These testimonies are the highest reward imaginable for a team dedicated to the preservation and wellbeing of these magnificent animals.

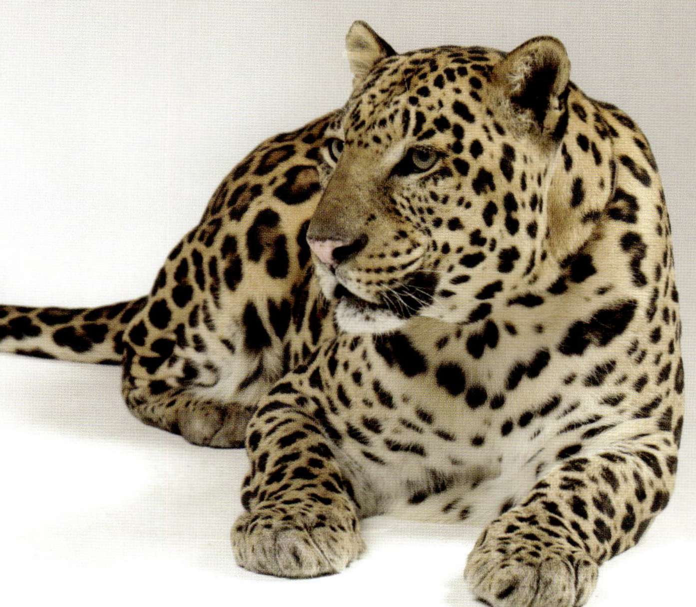

NATURE'S MASTERPIECE

Of all the beautiful and exotic creatures that call the preserve home, the tigers will always be the main attraction. Tigers are the monarchs of nature. A part of ourselves reflects back from a tiger's eyes: a dimension of our being that disappeared into memory long ago. It is not unusual to see guests at the preserve cry over this remembrance of how the world once was. The contrast between the purity in a tiger's eyes and the clutter of everyday life is stunning.

We asked ourselves how we could convey the impact of such moments to people who have never visited the preserve, and that is how this book came to be. To maximize the experience of meeting big cats face-to-face we built an all-white photography studio on the grounds of the preserve. By photographing the animals against a stark white background, we sought to assure that nothing would interfere with seeing their vibrant form, bold markings and striking individual personalities.

Being physically present before a tiger stimulates deep feelings of appreciation for a natural world. That feeling is enhanced even more when you meet one of the brilliantly colourful Royal white or Golden tabby tigers; or when you are face-to-face with unique varieties such as the Snow tiger. Big cats with such vibrant and varied colours no longer exist in the wild, and the preserve exists to help protect the few remaining descendants of these regal families from complete annihilation.

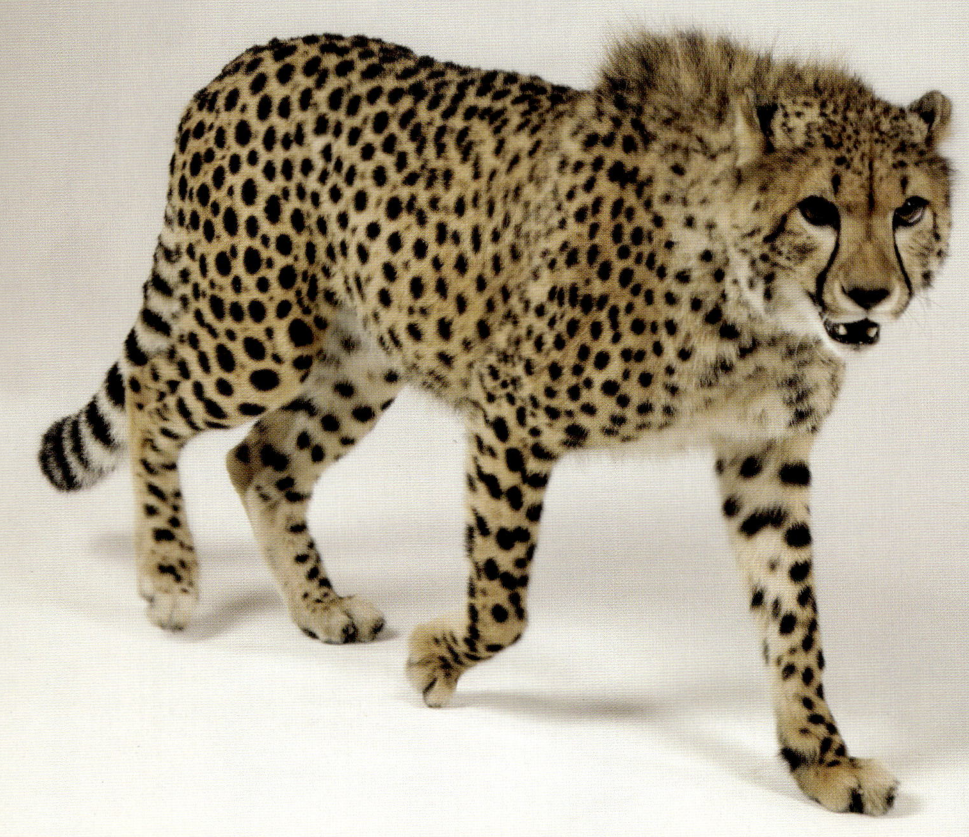

I wish there were some way of describing what it is like to be with tigers. The sensation might best be described as a feeling of awe. The greatness of tigers emanates from their powerful spirit or what ancient dwellers in the Himalayan mountains call *Shaktipat*: the kinetic energy of the universe. You feel that energy when you are in their presence. You feel as though you have been spiritual and mentally stimulated. Tigers live in the moment, and being with the tigers focuses your thoughts. In their physical company you no longer dwell in the past or worry about the future. Tigers ground us in the moment.

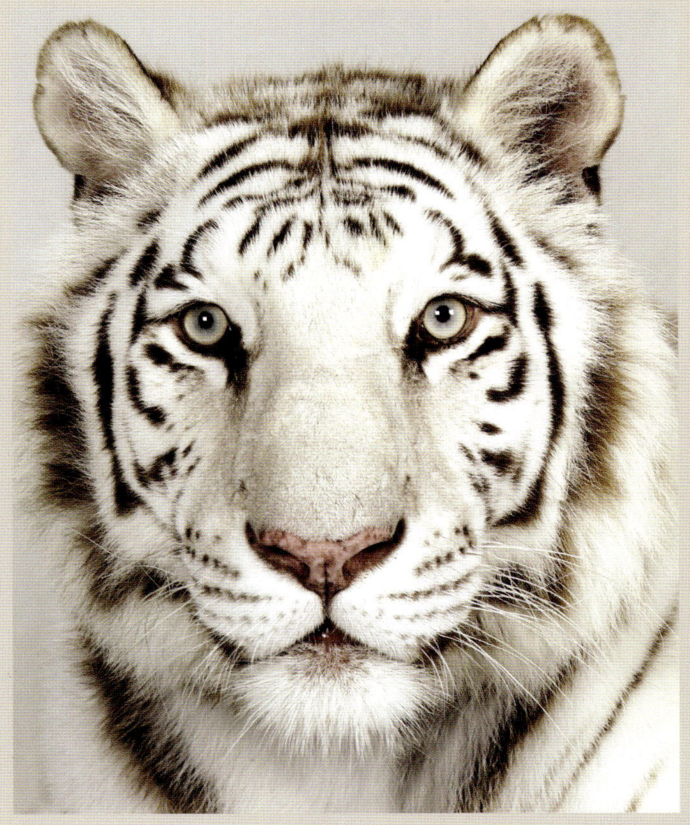

FADING INTO MEMORY

In a world beset by environmental challenges and the projected loss of one-third of all species within the next fifty years (according to the Intergovernmental Panel on Climate Change), why do big cats deserve special attention? Big cats are at the very top of the proverbial food chain. Their wellbeing safeguards the wellbeing of hundreds of other species. Big cats are a barometer of the health and vitality of the whole jungle. The ripple effect from losing the big cat population would be felt across the entire spectrum of animal life.

The plight of big cats is an environmental emergency. Today less than one percent is left of the many varieties that once roamed the earth, and the remaining population is being killed off at an alarming rate. Our children and grandchildren may soon live in a world where tigers and other beautiful creatures will only be memories. T.I.G.E.R.S. Preserve is helping to improve those odds with interactive environments that serve as refuge, birthing centre and tiger resort. As one journal described, 'T.I.G.E.R.S. is like a zoo times a zillion.'

The book you are holding was prepared with two purposes in mind: to provide readers with a taste of the unique experience of meeting big cats in person, and to serve as an invitation to visit and help to preserve these magnificent animals for generations to come. For those who have visited T.I.G.E.R.S., this book is an extension of that live encounter. For those who have not yet visited, here is an intimate look at the most beautiful creatures on the planet – along with our invitation to come see them in person. You are welcome to visit us. There is something unique waiting for you, which can transform the way you see yourself and the world around you forever.

'Doc' Bhagavan Antle, August 2009

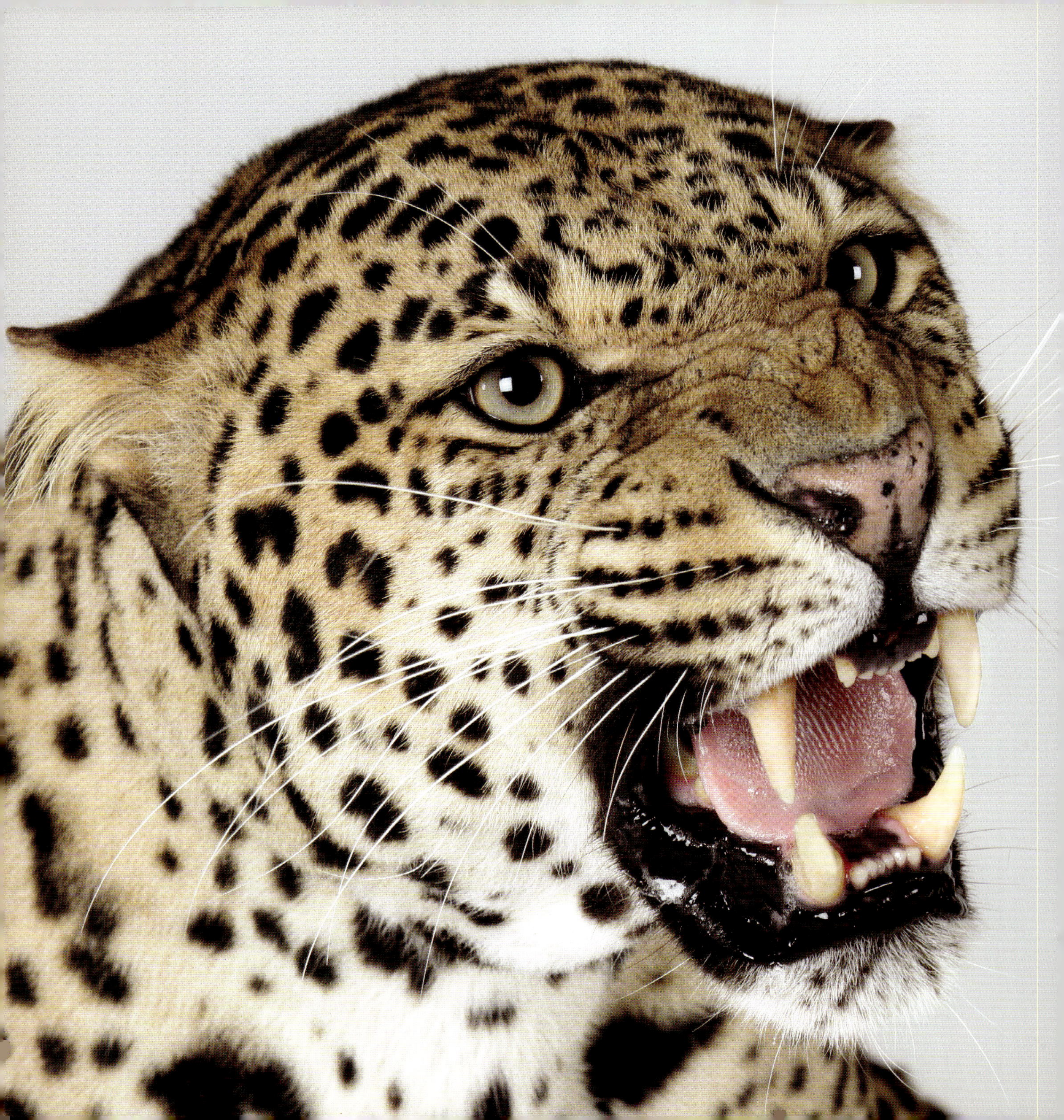

LEOPARD

The leopard is the smallest cat of the 'big four' and has the largest distribution worldwide – from as far north as Siberia to South Africa. With its short legs and long body, the leopard is a successful hunter and is particularly adept at climbing trees. Known for its varied hunting techniques and surprising speed, the leopard will hunt and kill animals much larger than itself. Using its powerful jaw to lift heavy prey, the leopard can grow up to 5¼ft (1.6m) from head to tail and weigh up to 200lb (91kg). Generally solitary creatures, leopards spend much of their time in trees and prefer to hunt at night, tending to avoid any contact with humans. However, there have been notorious cases of man-eating leopards, especially in India.

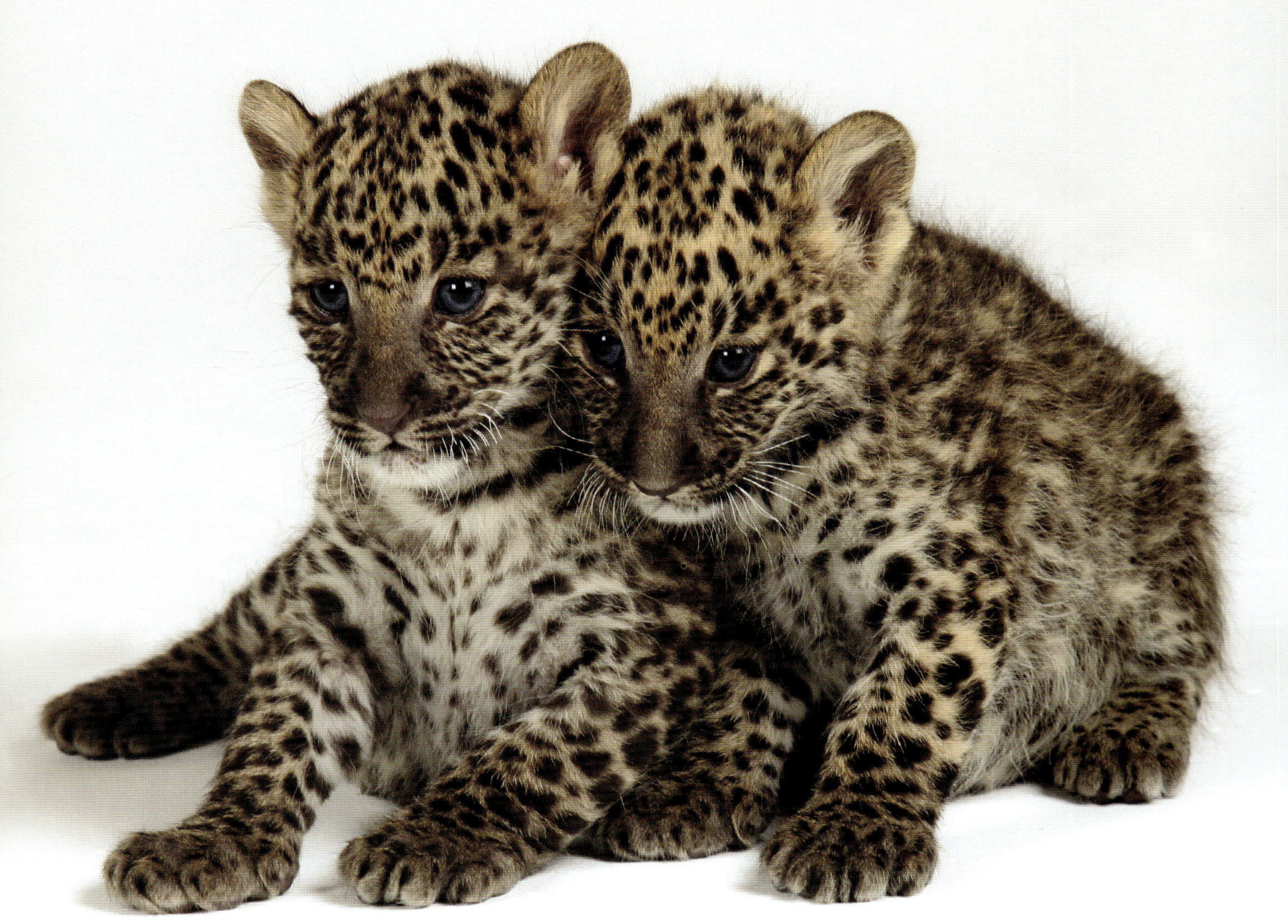

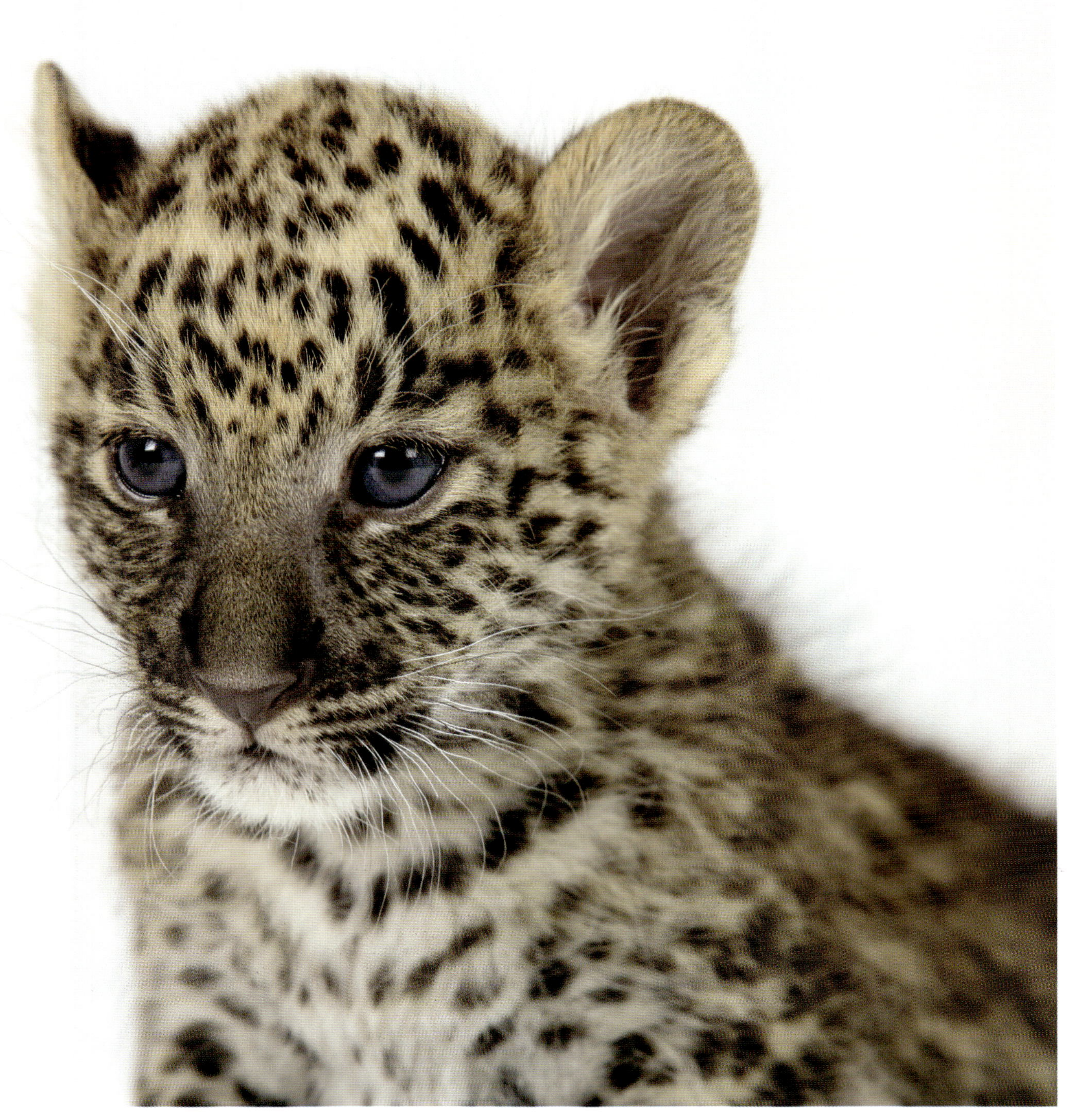

The fur of young leopards tends to be longer, thicker and more grey in colour than that of adults.

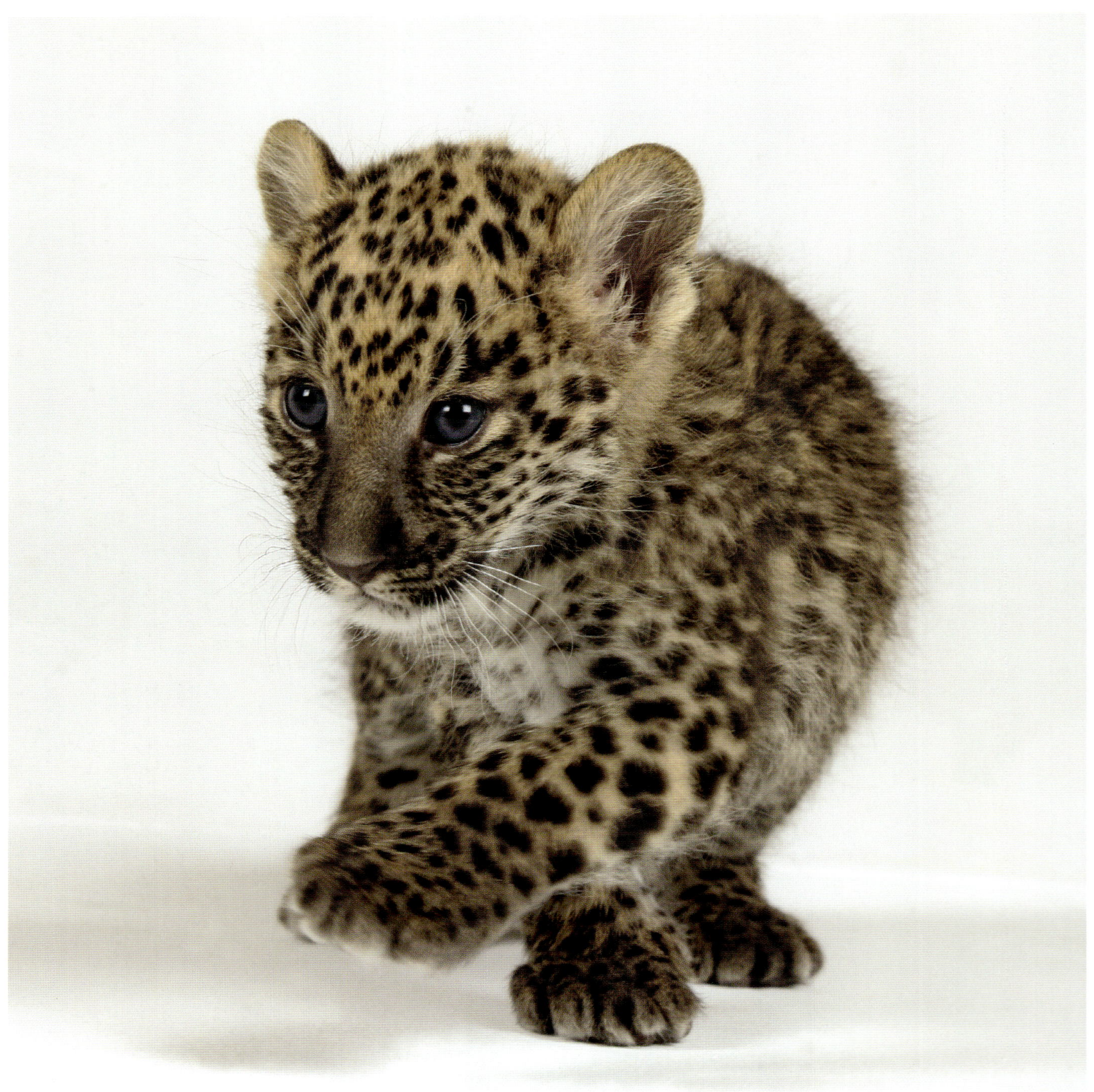

Leopard cubs remain with their mother for 18–24 months after birth.

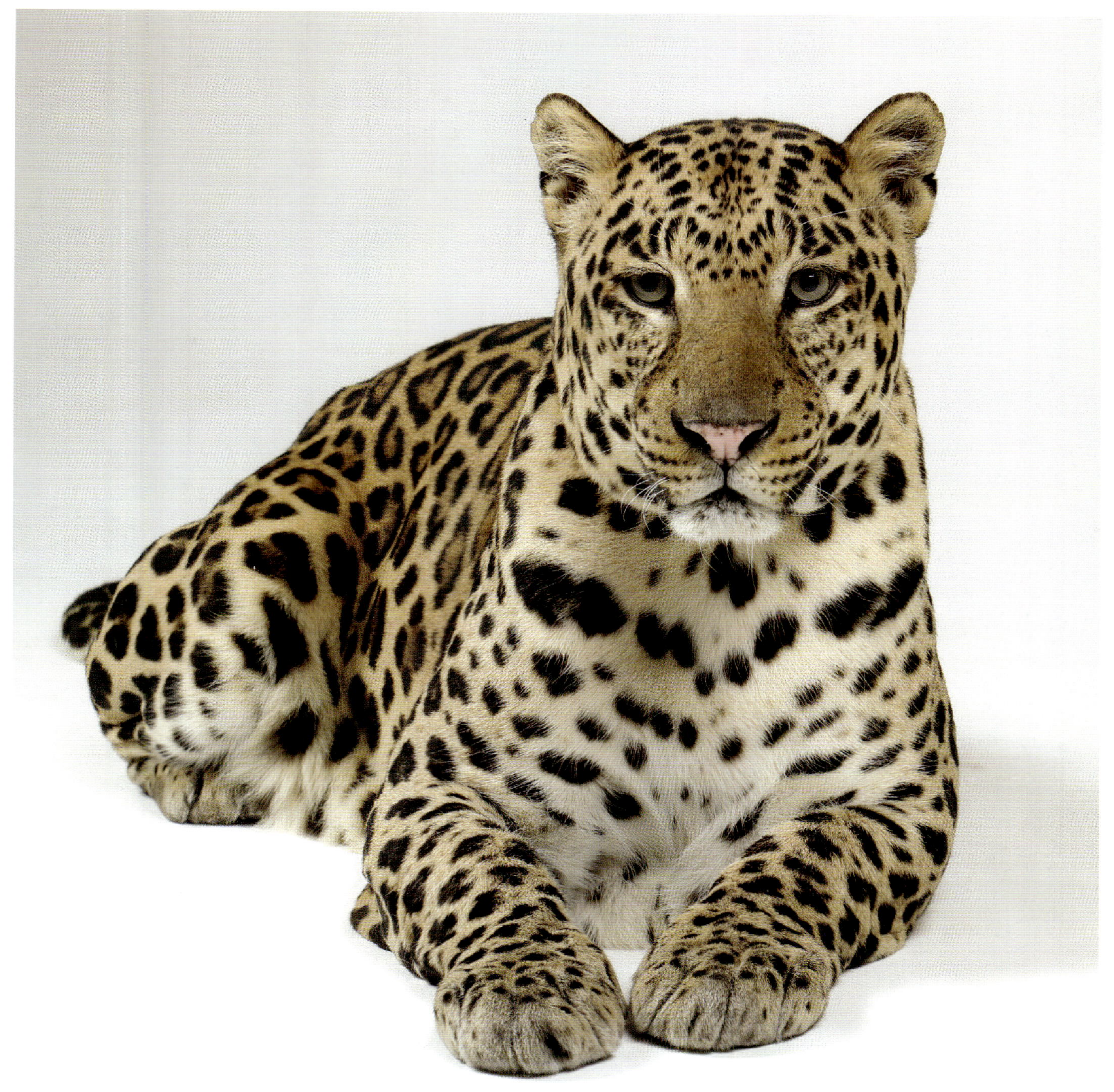

The leopard is the smartest of the big cats. It makes up for its relatively small size with brain power.

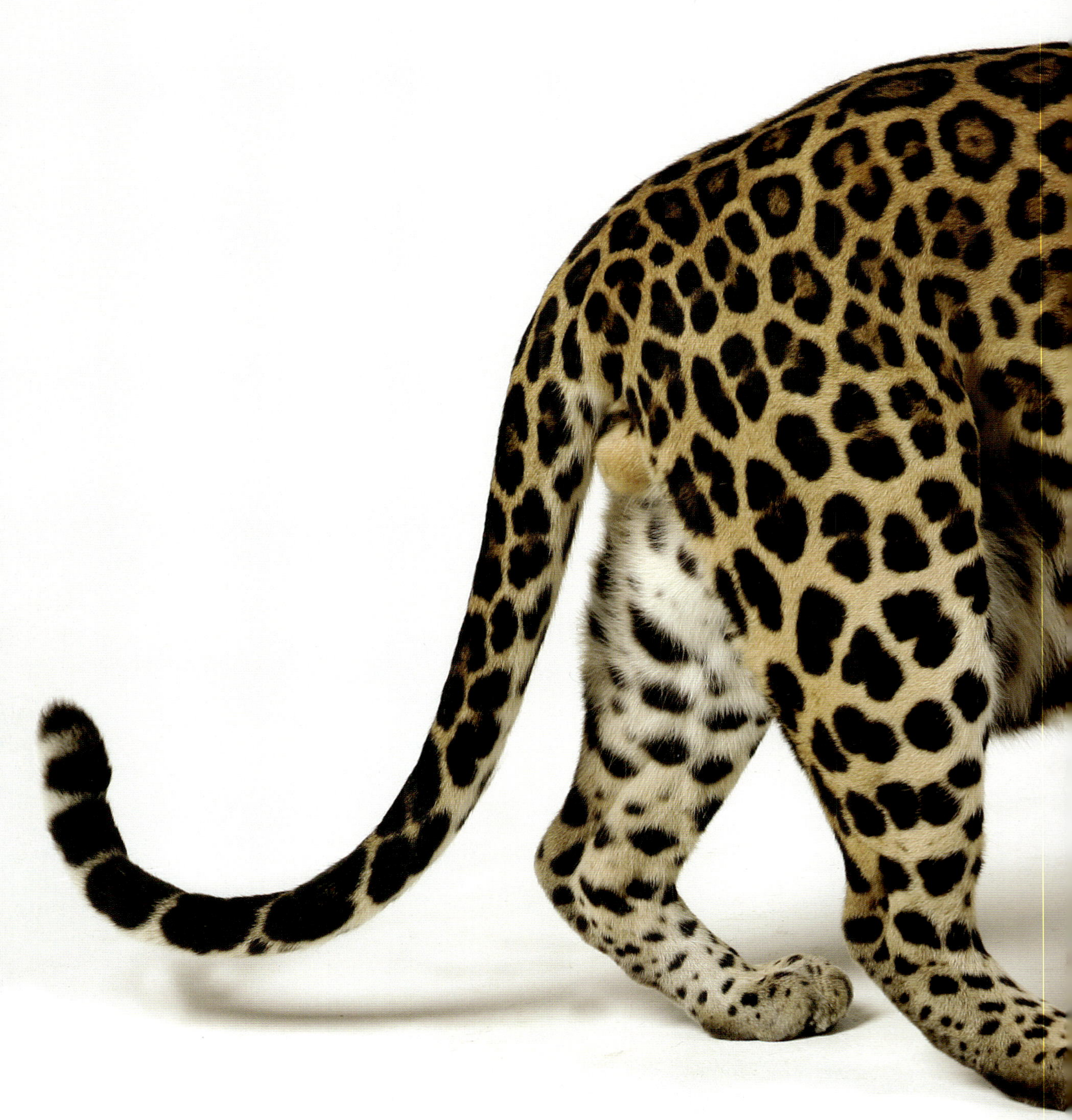

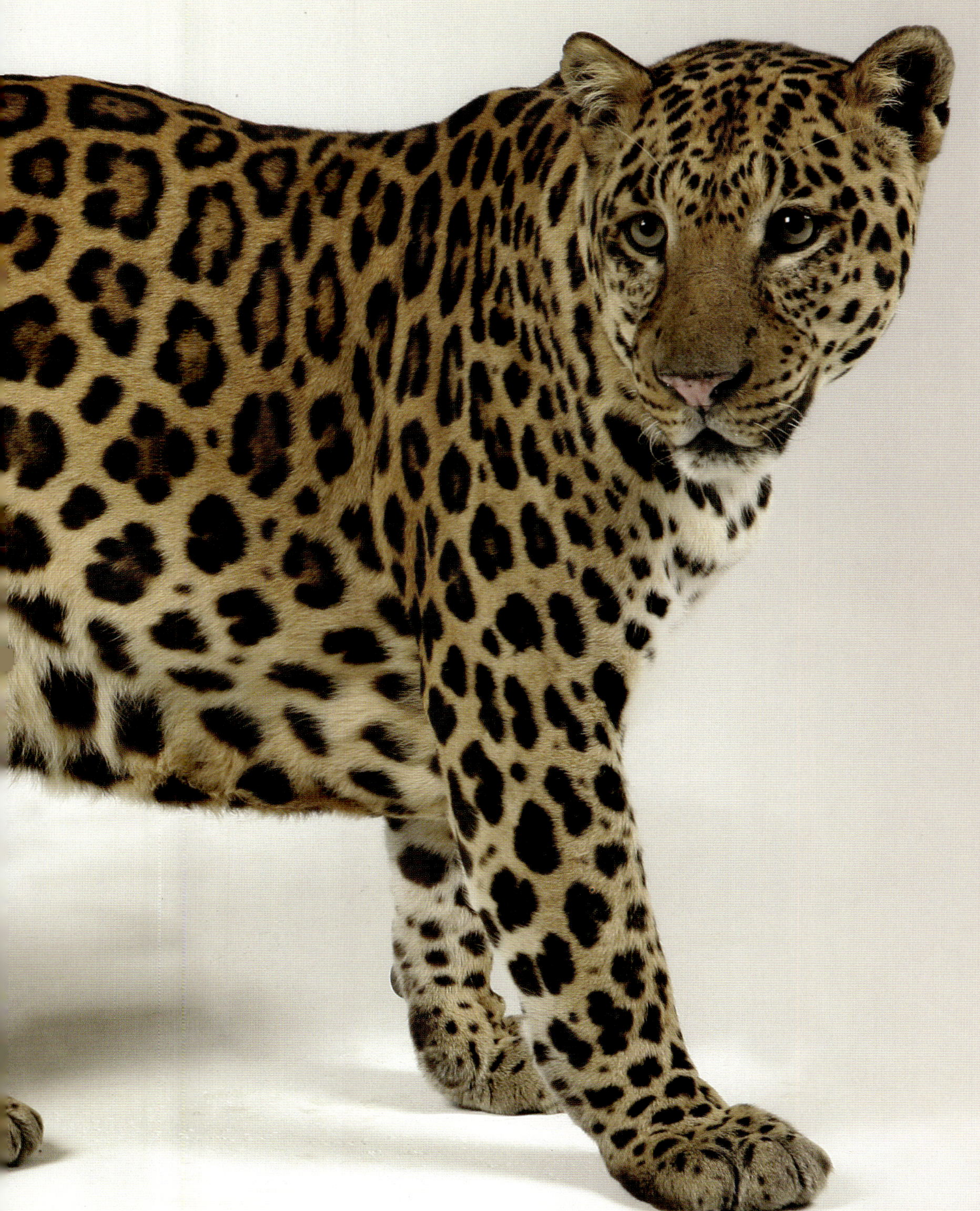

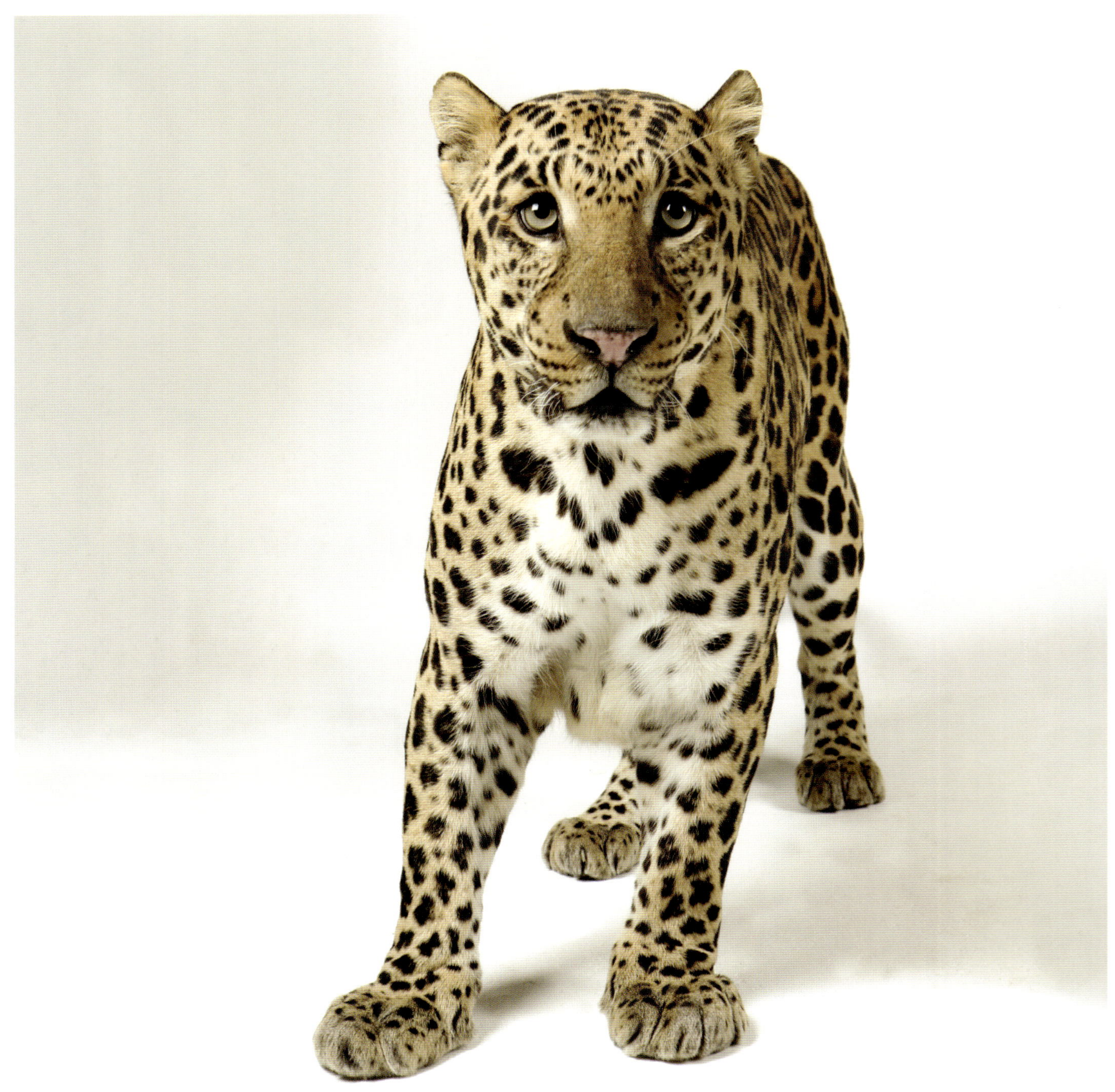

Leopards are very adaptive animals, able to quickly discern patterns which helps them to hunt a wide variety of prey.

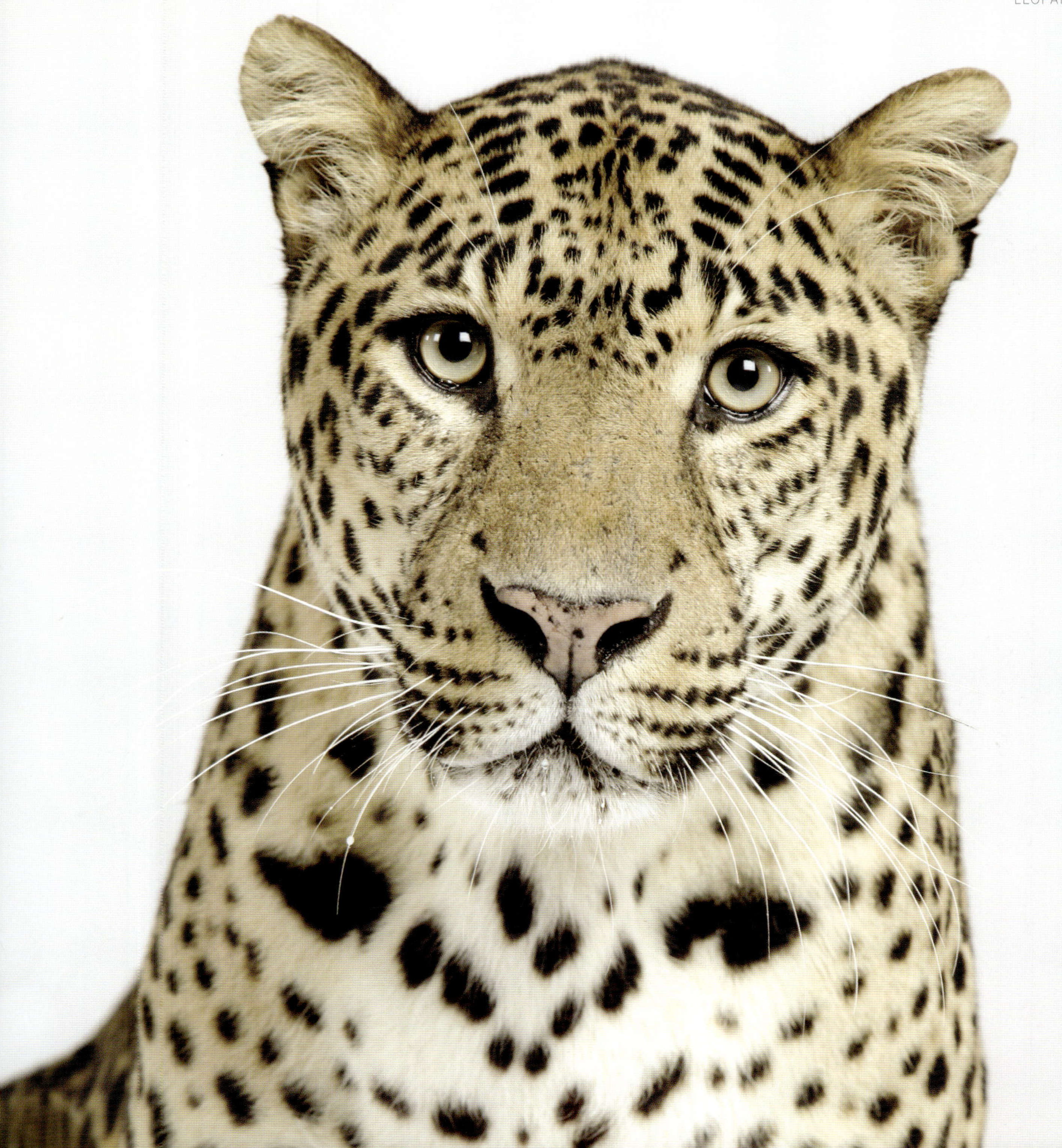

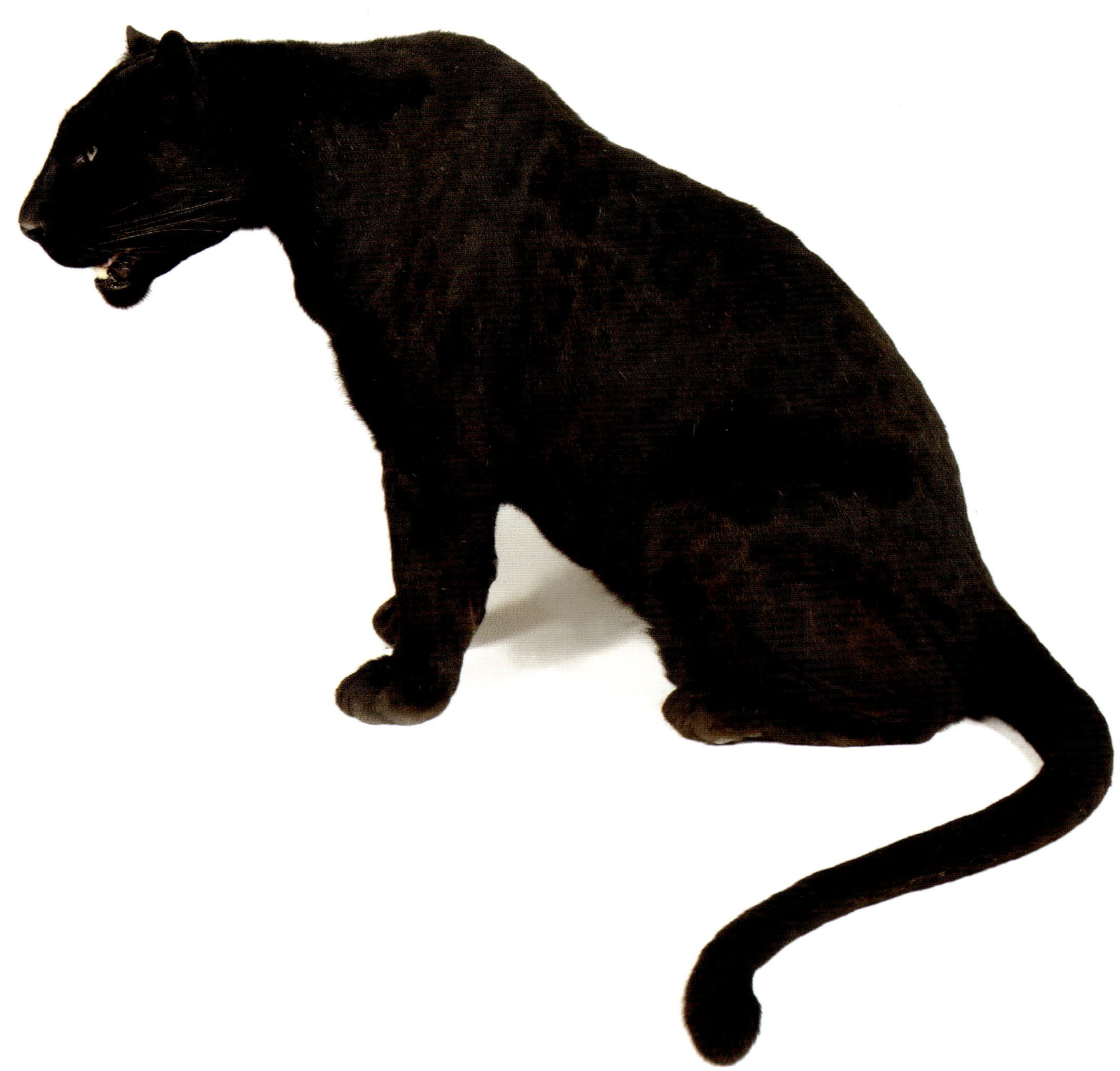

The colouring of black (melanistic) leopards is caused by a recessive gene and is more commonly found in areas of rainforest.

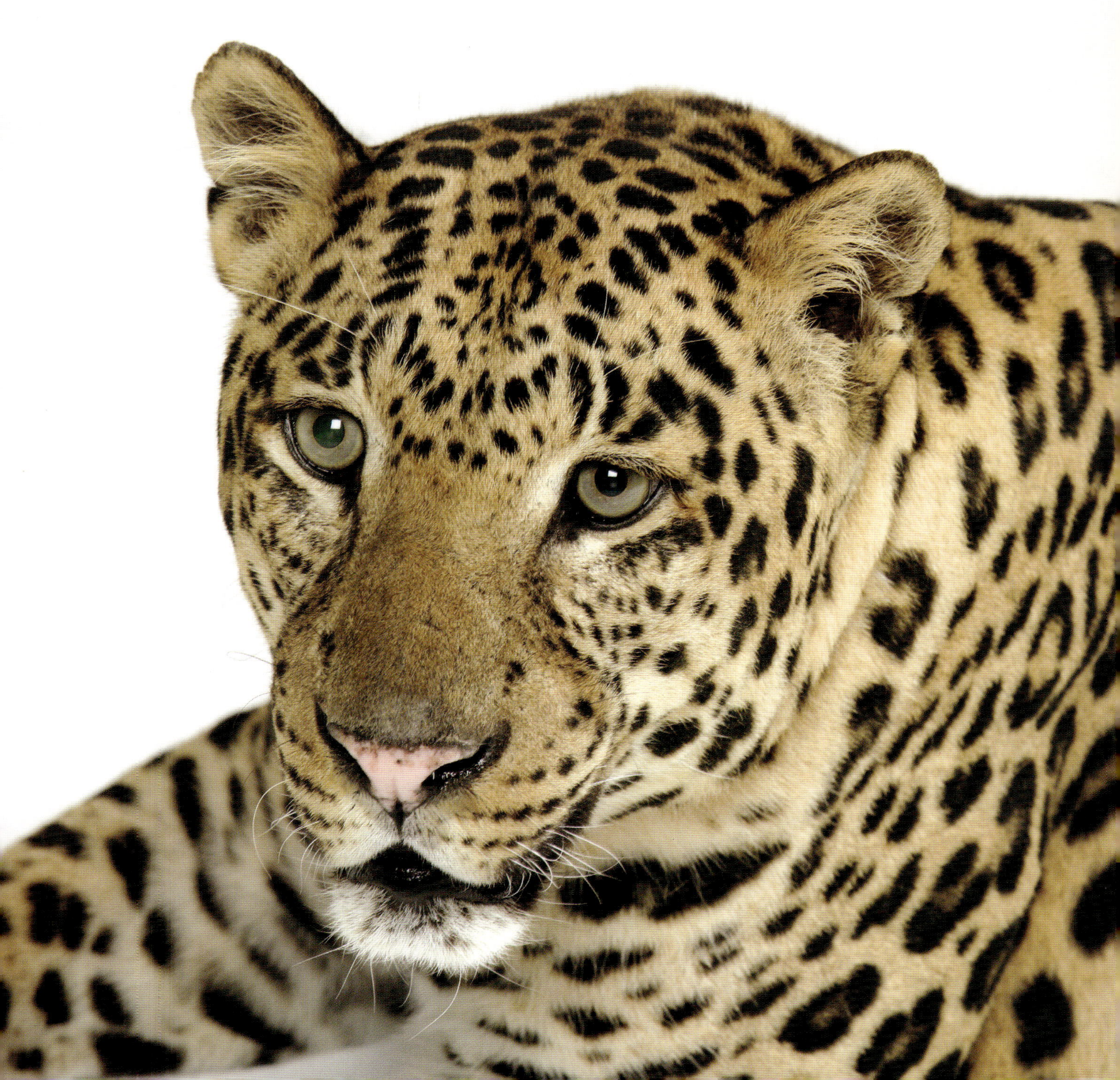

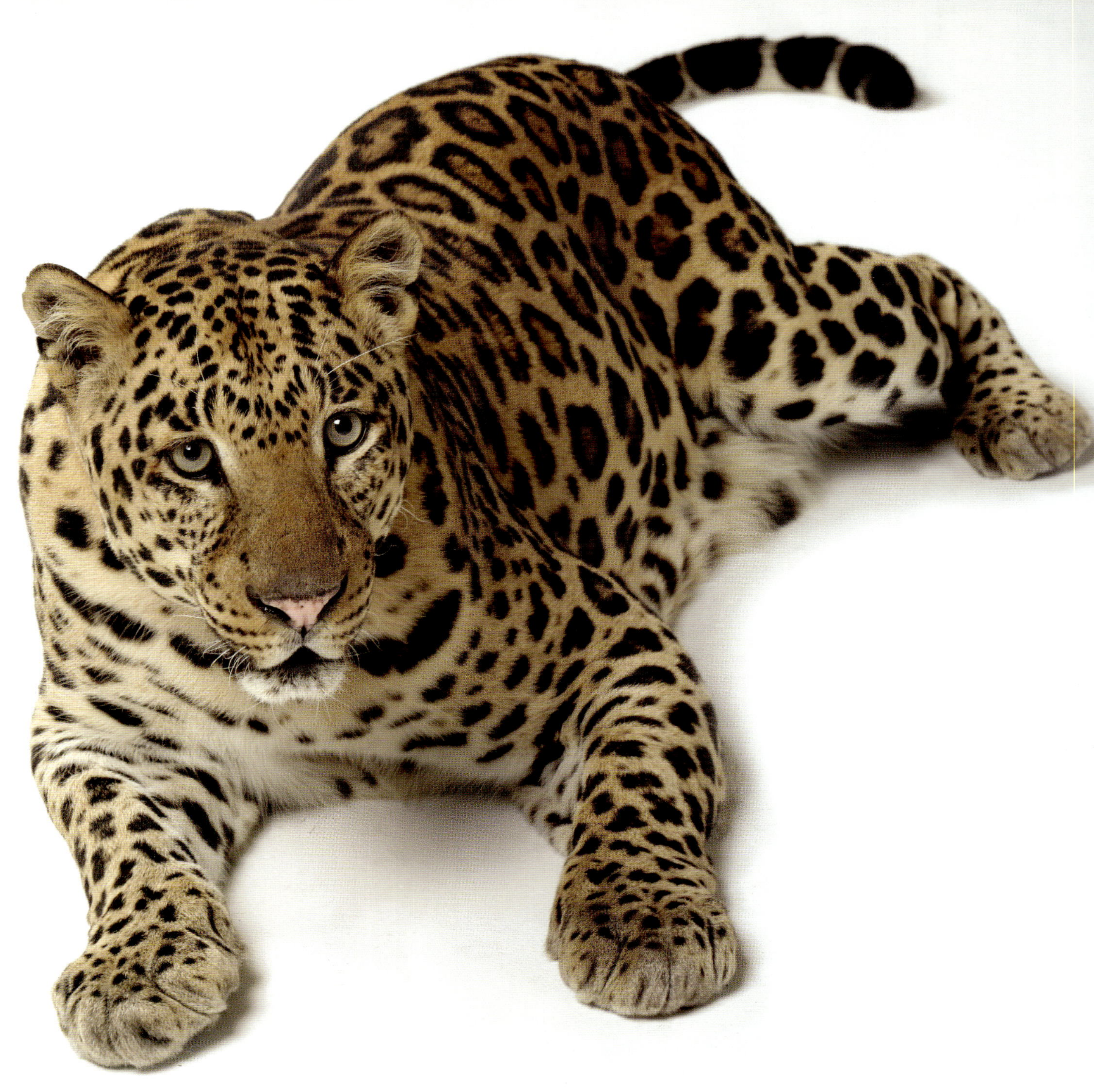

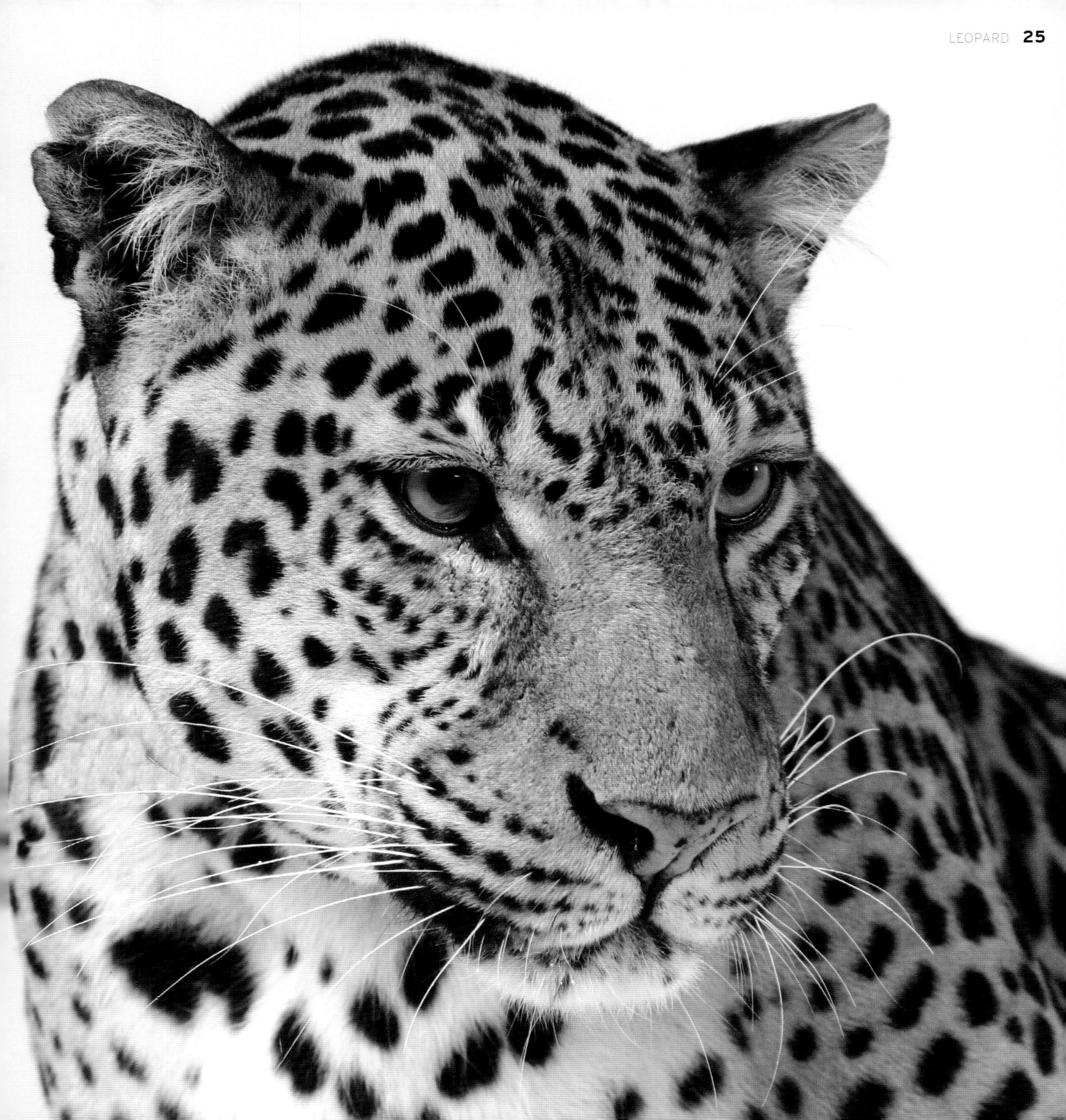

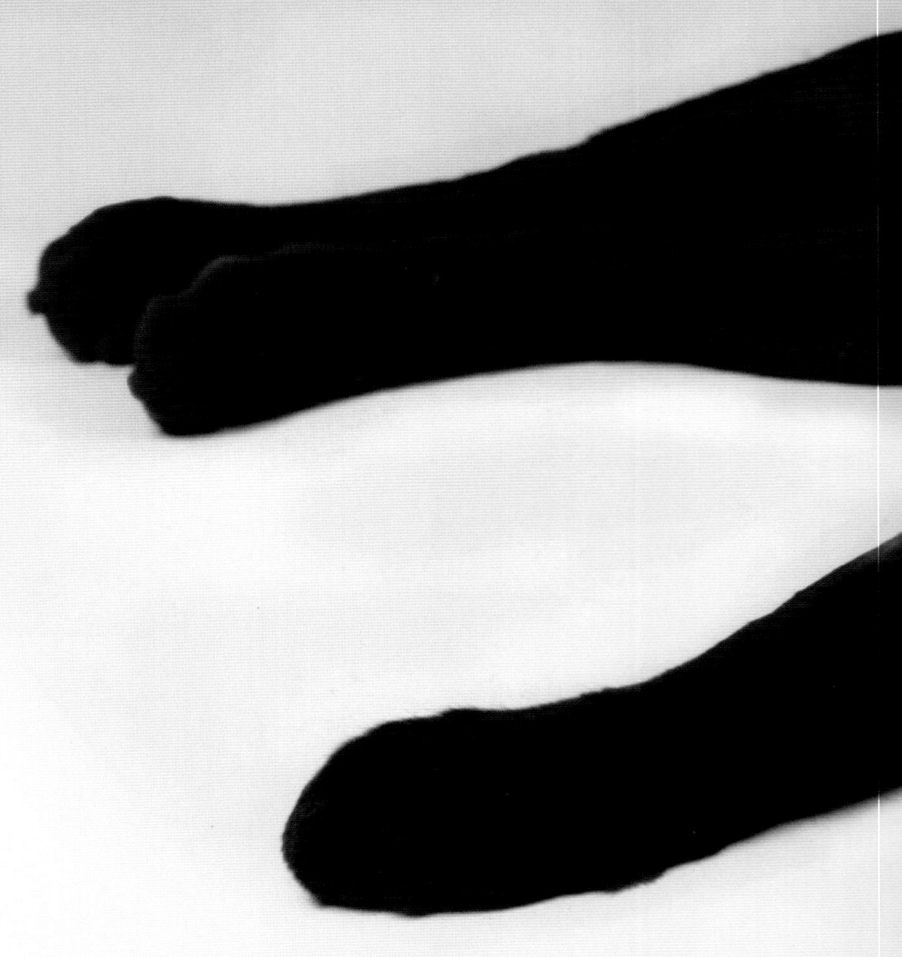

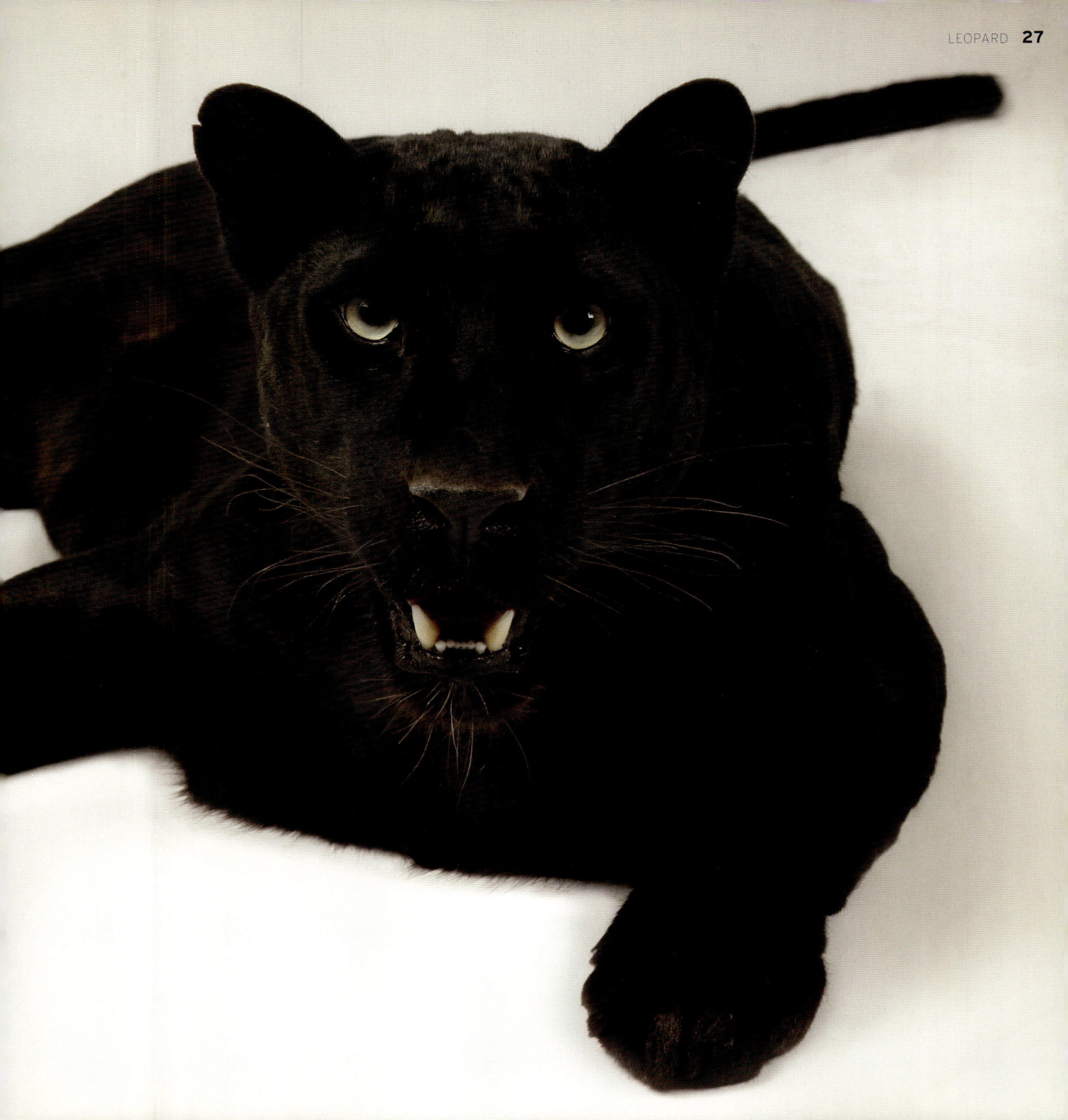

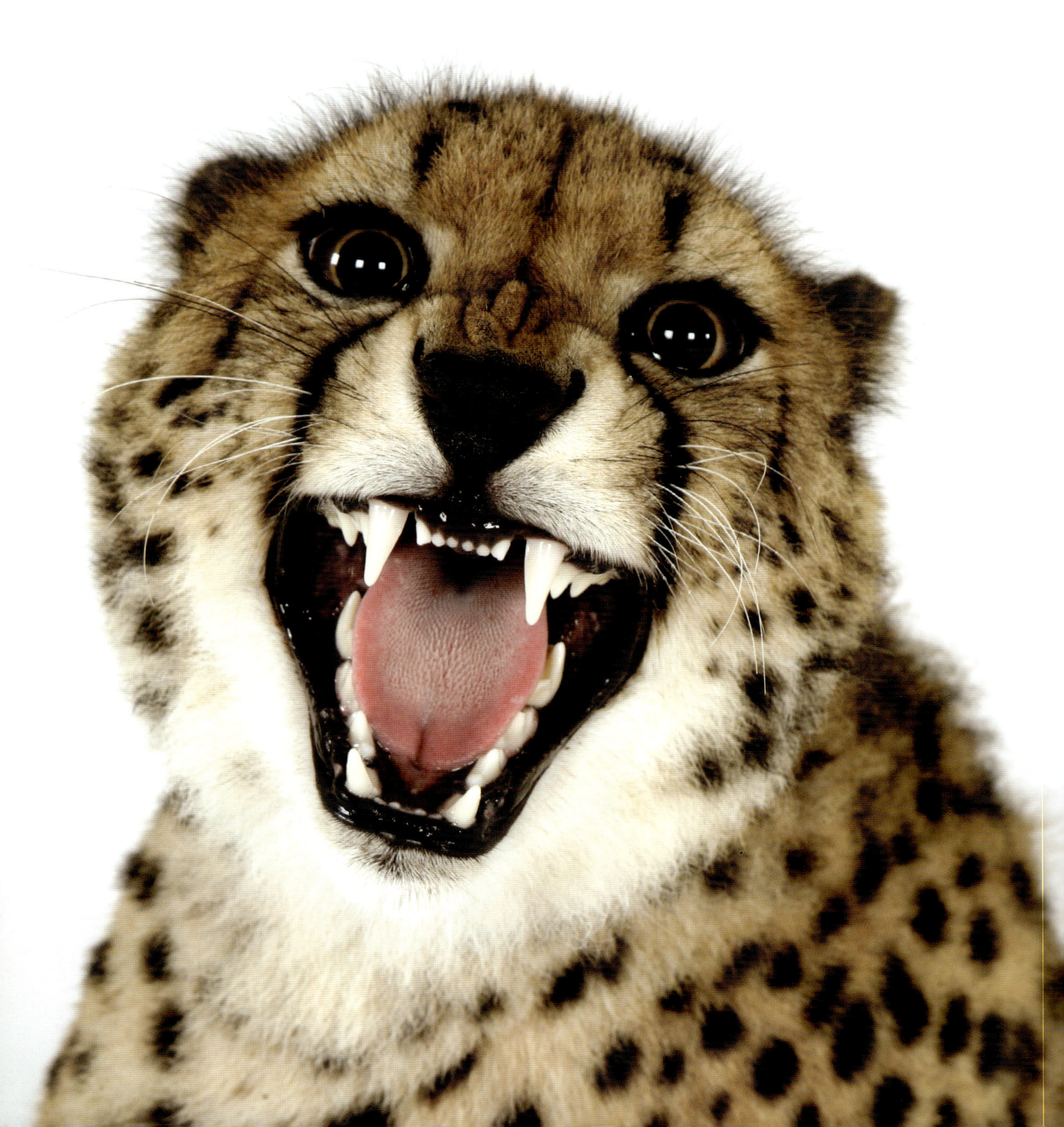

CHEETAH

Cheetahs were once found across the whole of Africa and as far to the east as India. There are now only isolated groups found in Africa and a small population in Iran. The cheetah population in the wild is estimated to be upwards of 12,000 and considered vulnerable to extinction. Known for their extreme acceleration, cheetahs are the fastest animals on land, capable of reaching speeds of up to 75mph (120kph). Designed for speed, they can grow up to 4½ft (1.3m) from head to tail and weigh up to 140lbs (63kg). Unlike most other big cats, the cheetah has enlarged nostrils, which allow for increased oxygen intake, and larger than average lungs and heart. They also have semi-retractable claws, which allow them greater grip and agility when chasing prey. They are sociable animals, banding together to protect a marked territory from larger cats.

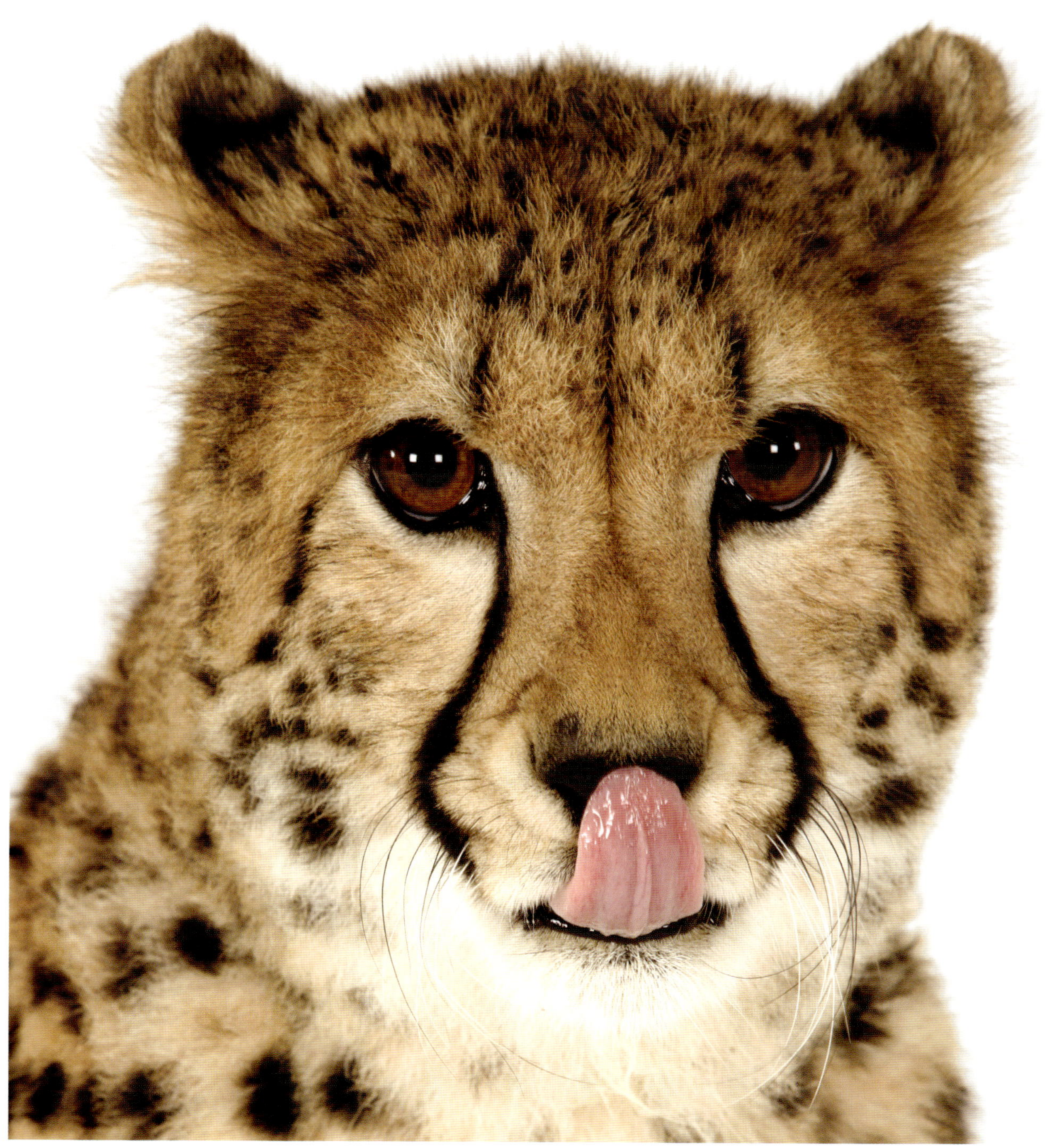

Black 'tear' marks run from the corner of a cheetah's eyes to keep sunlight out when hunting.

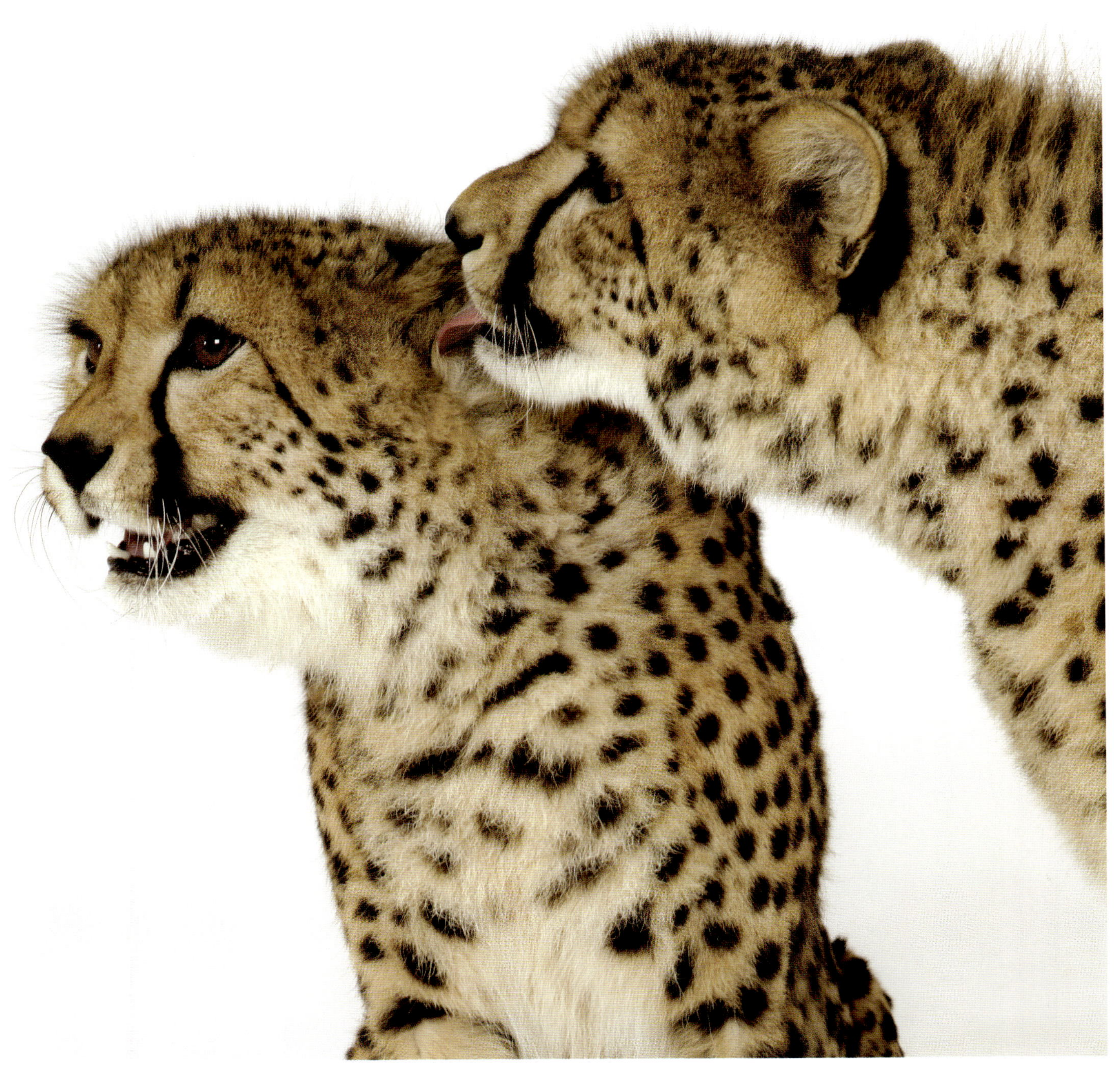

Cheetahs purr when they are content, usually during pleasant social meetings.

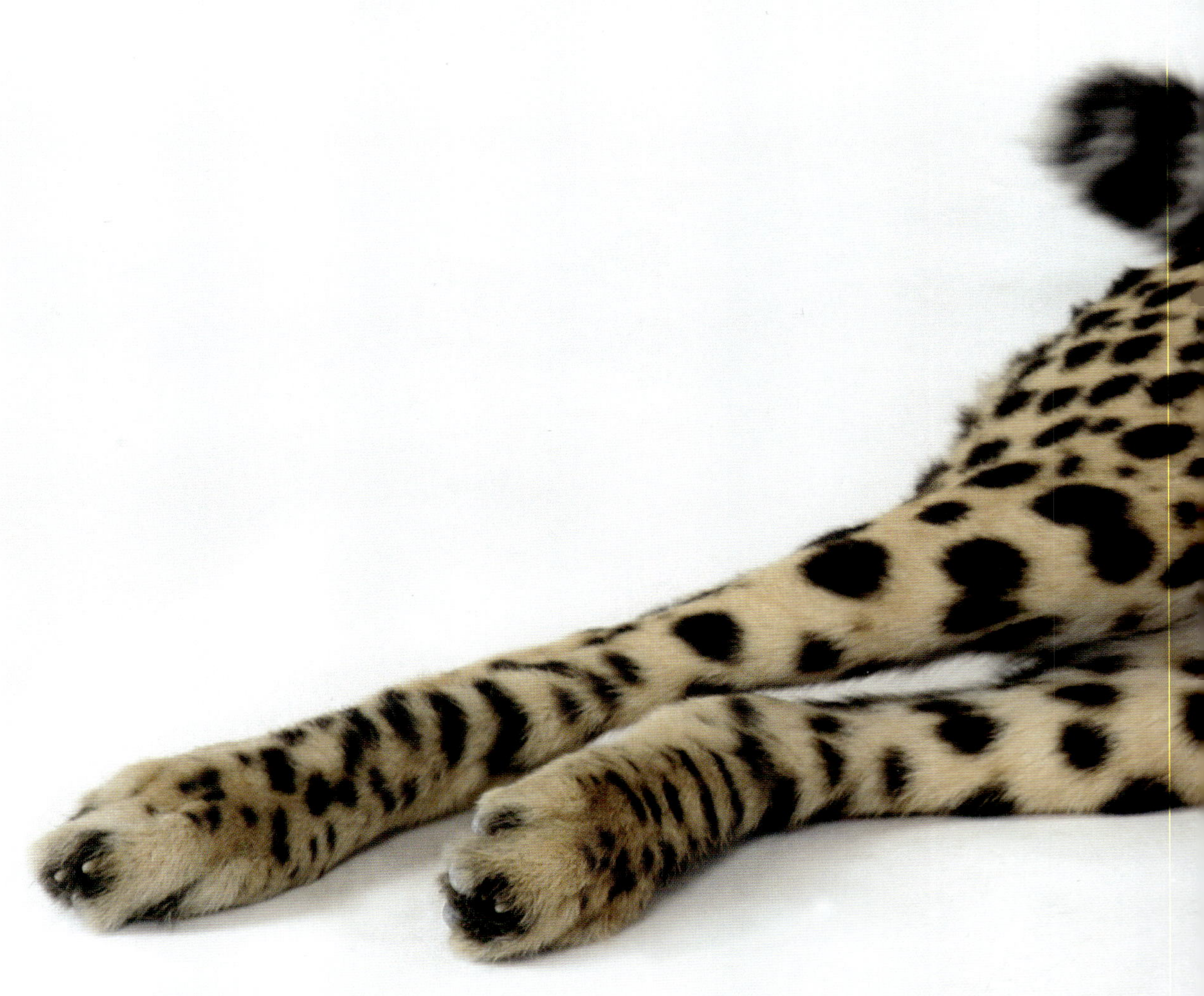

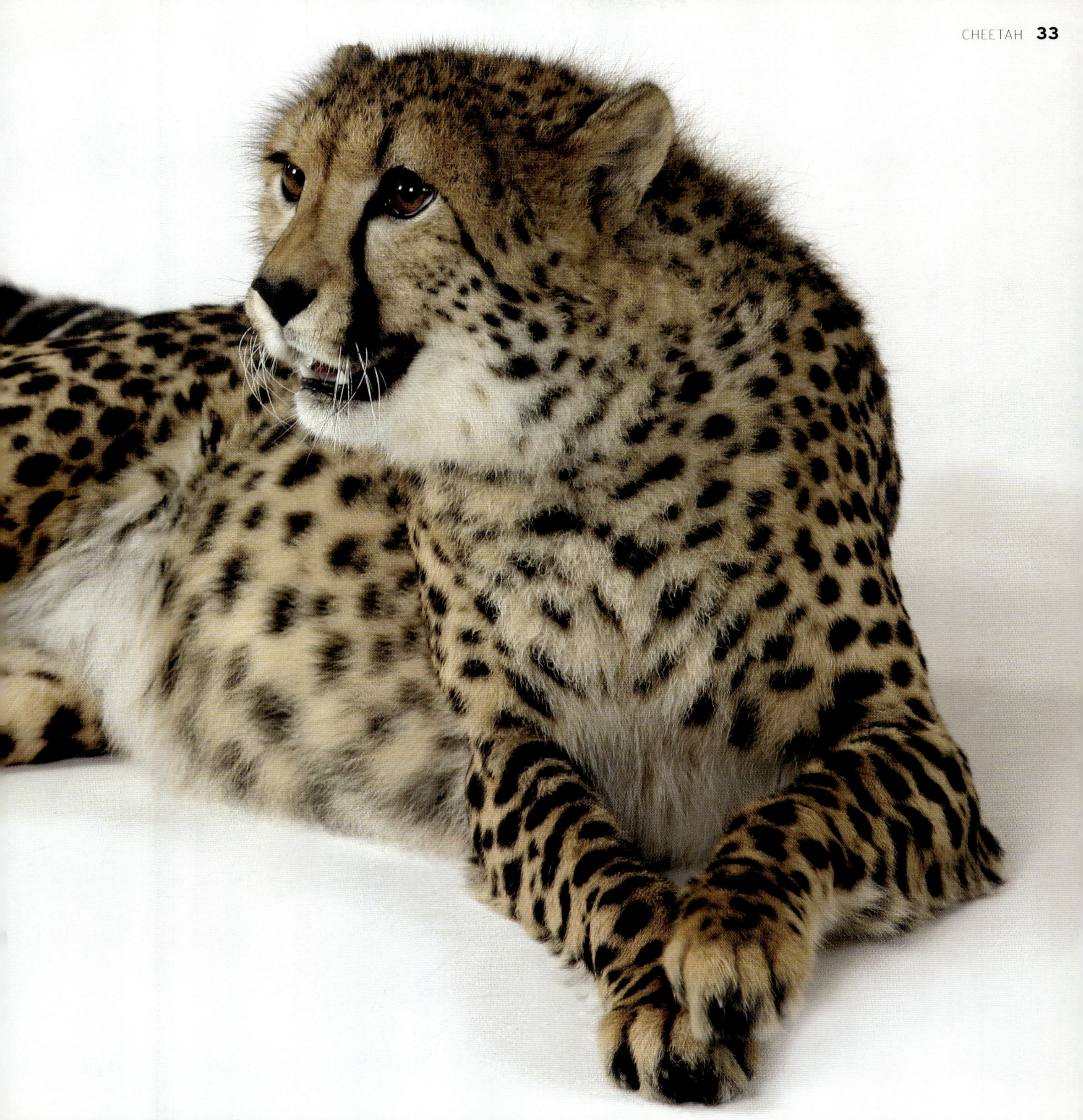

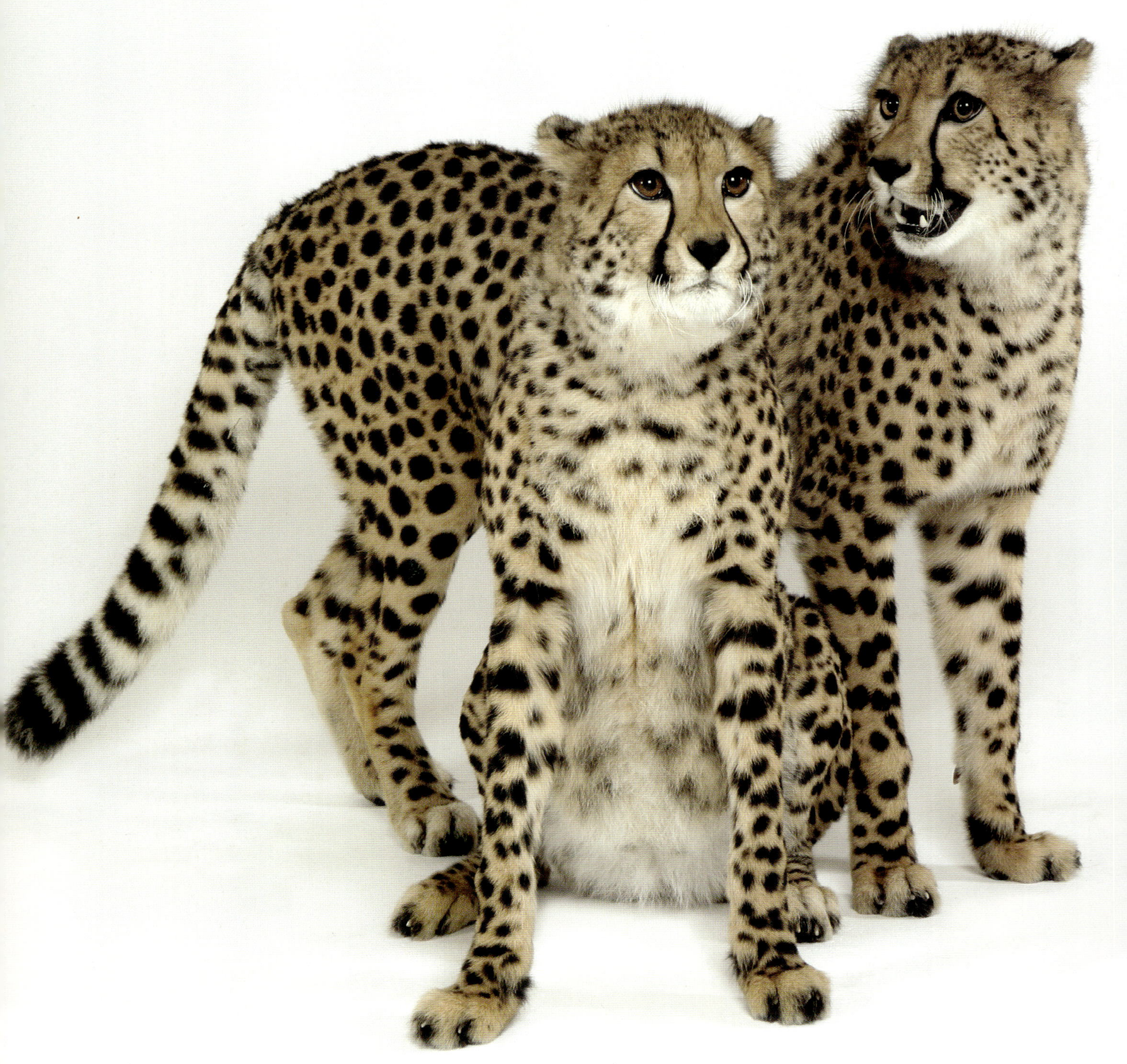

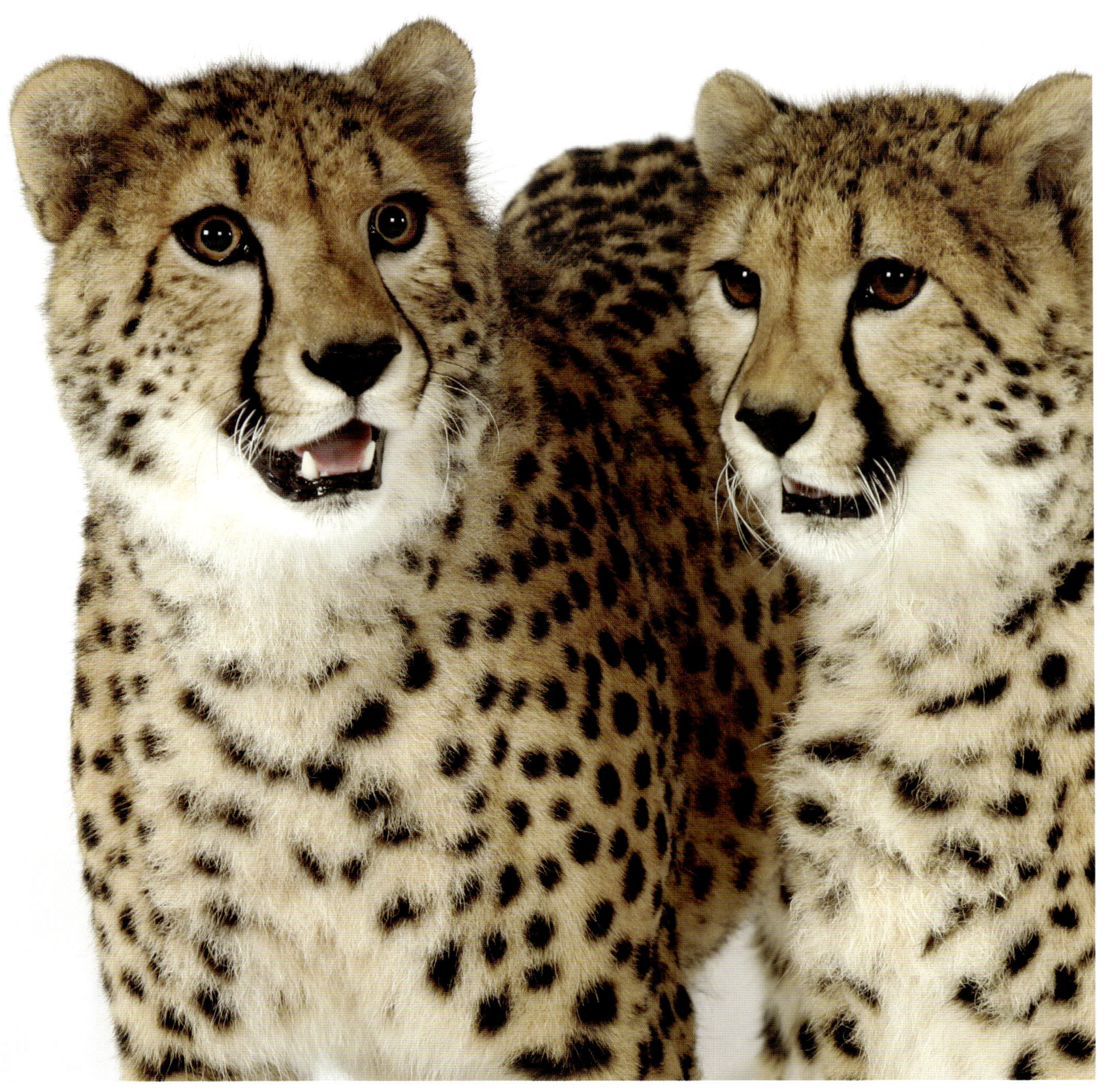

Cheetahs hunt by vision rather than by scent. They are nimble and selective predators.

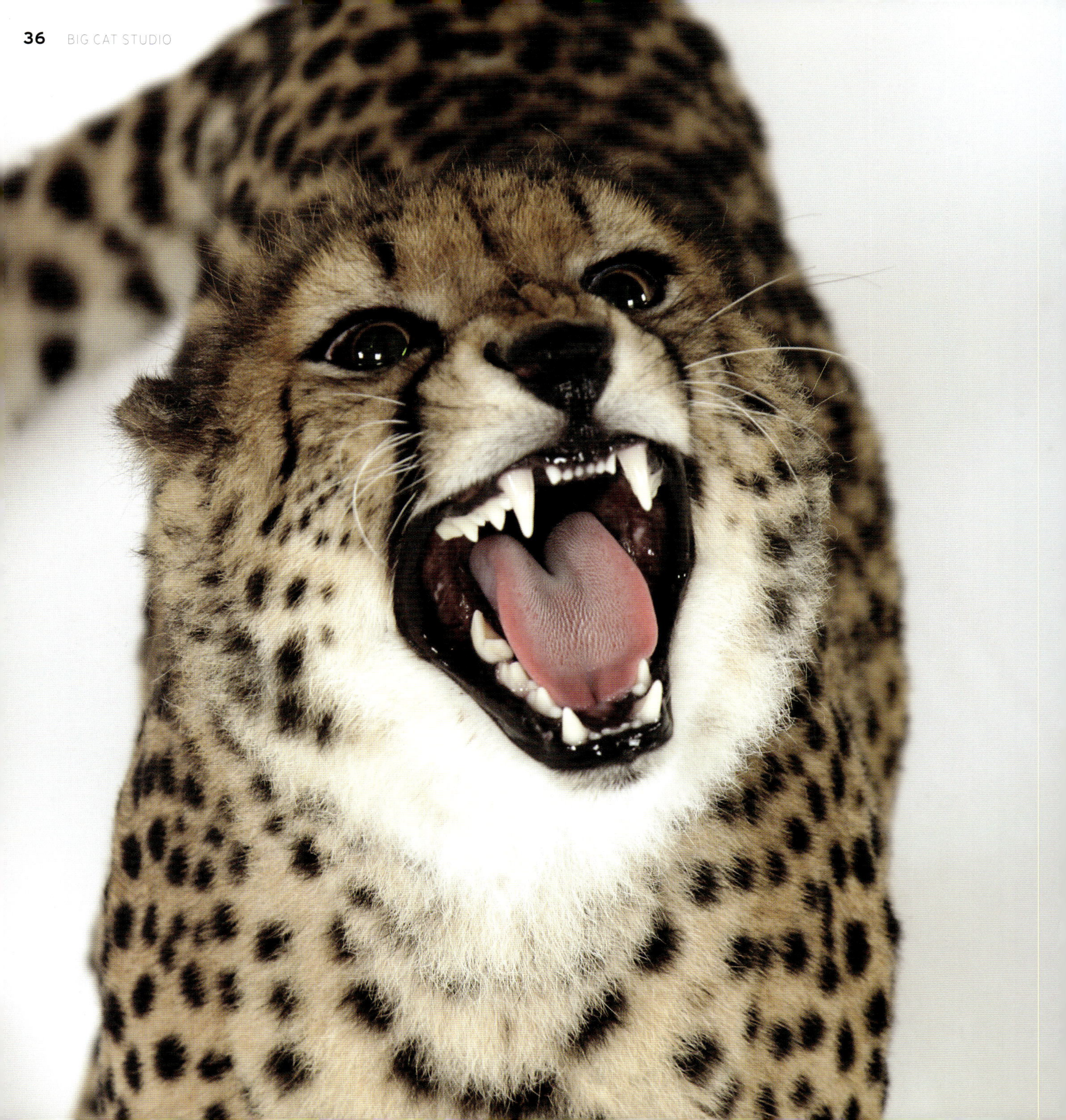

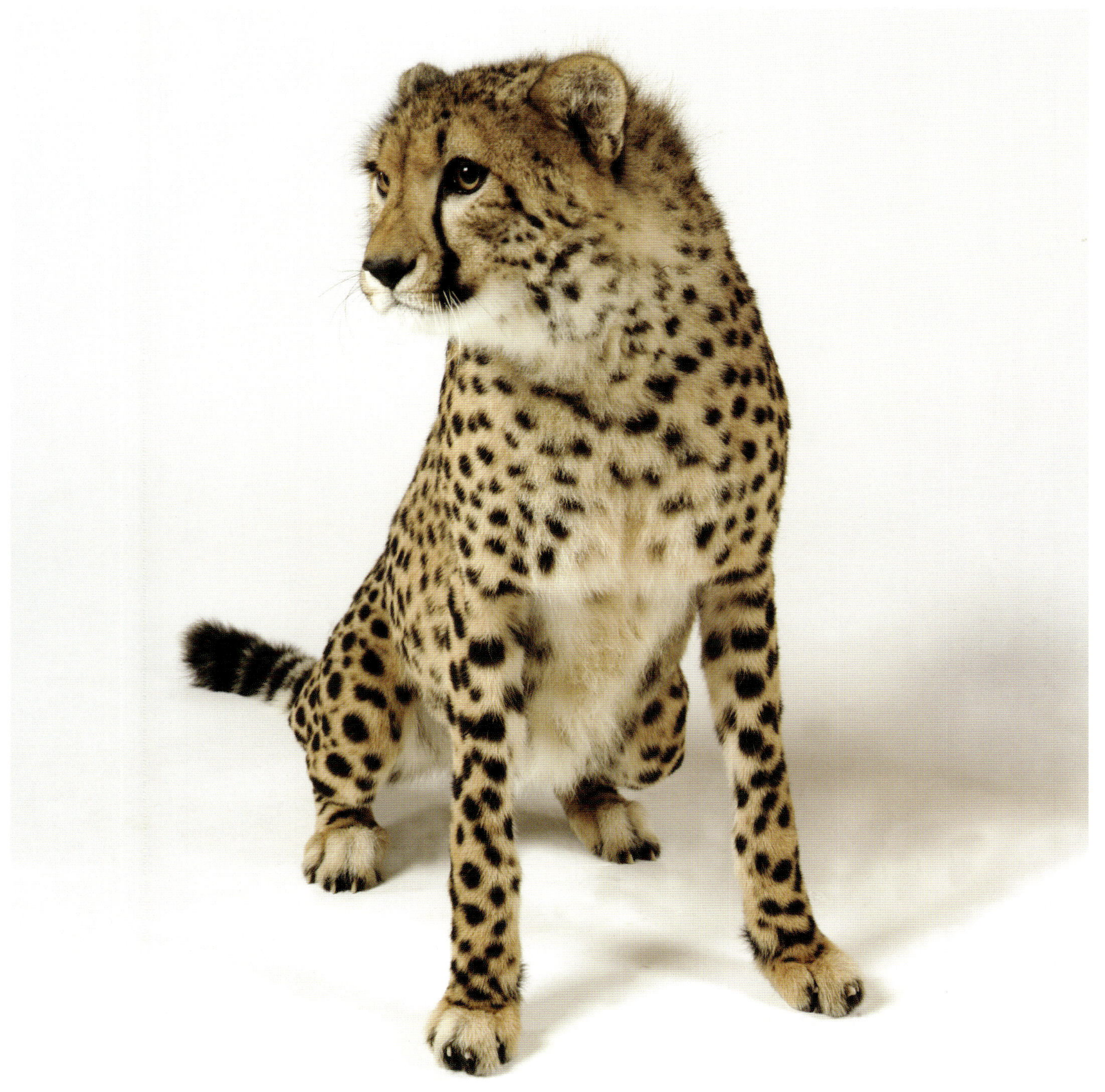

The diet of a cheetah depends upon the area in which it lives. They often feed on small gazelle on the African savannas.

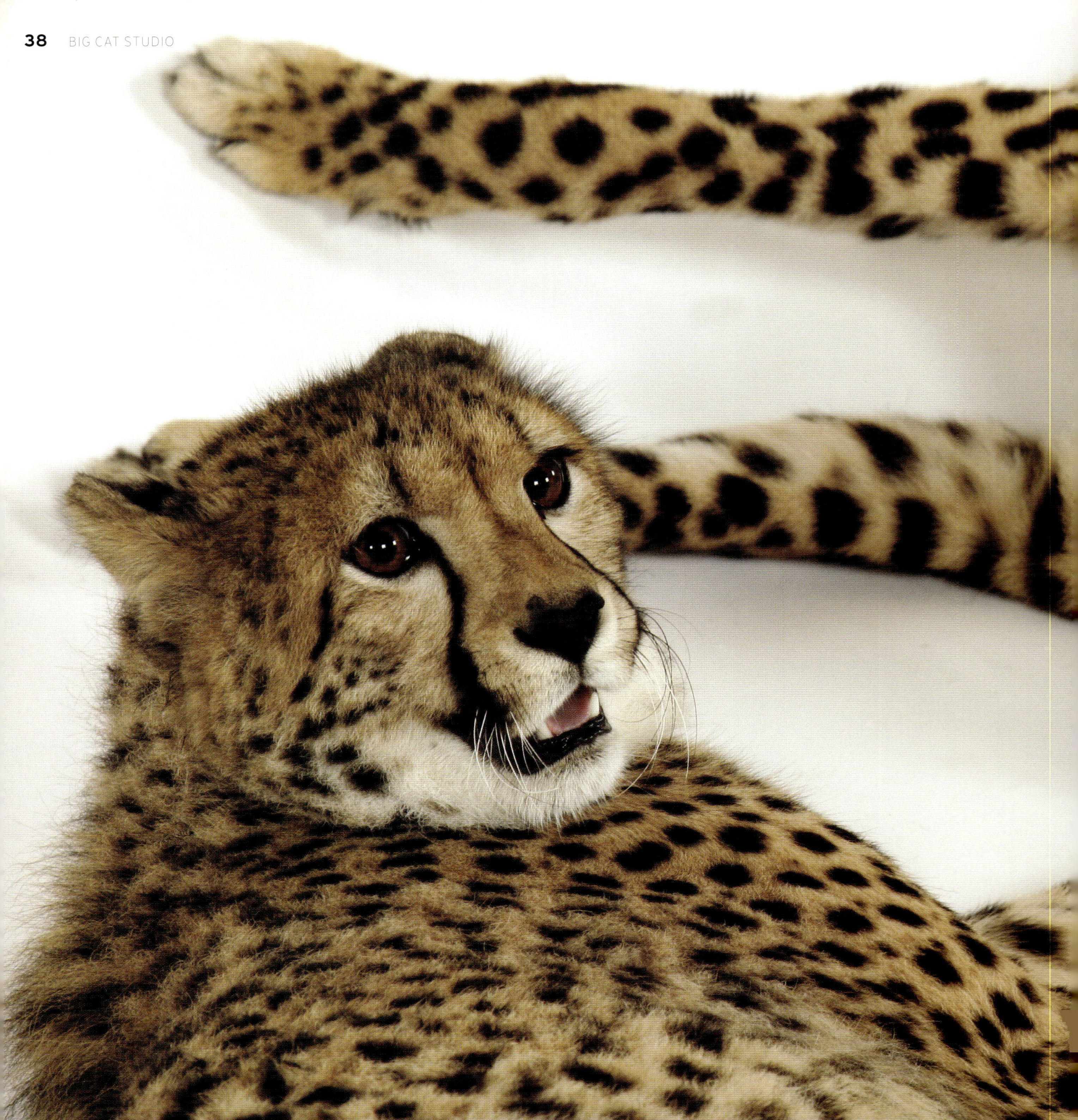

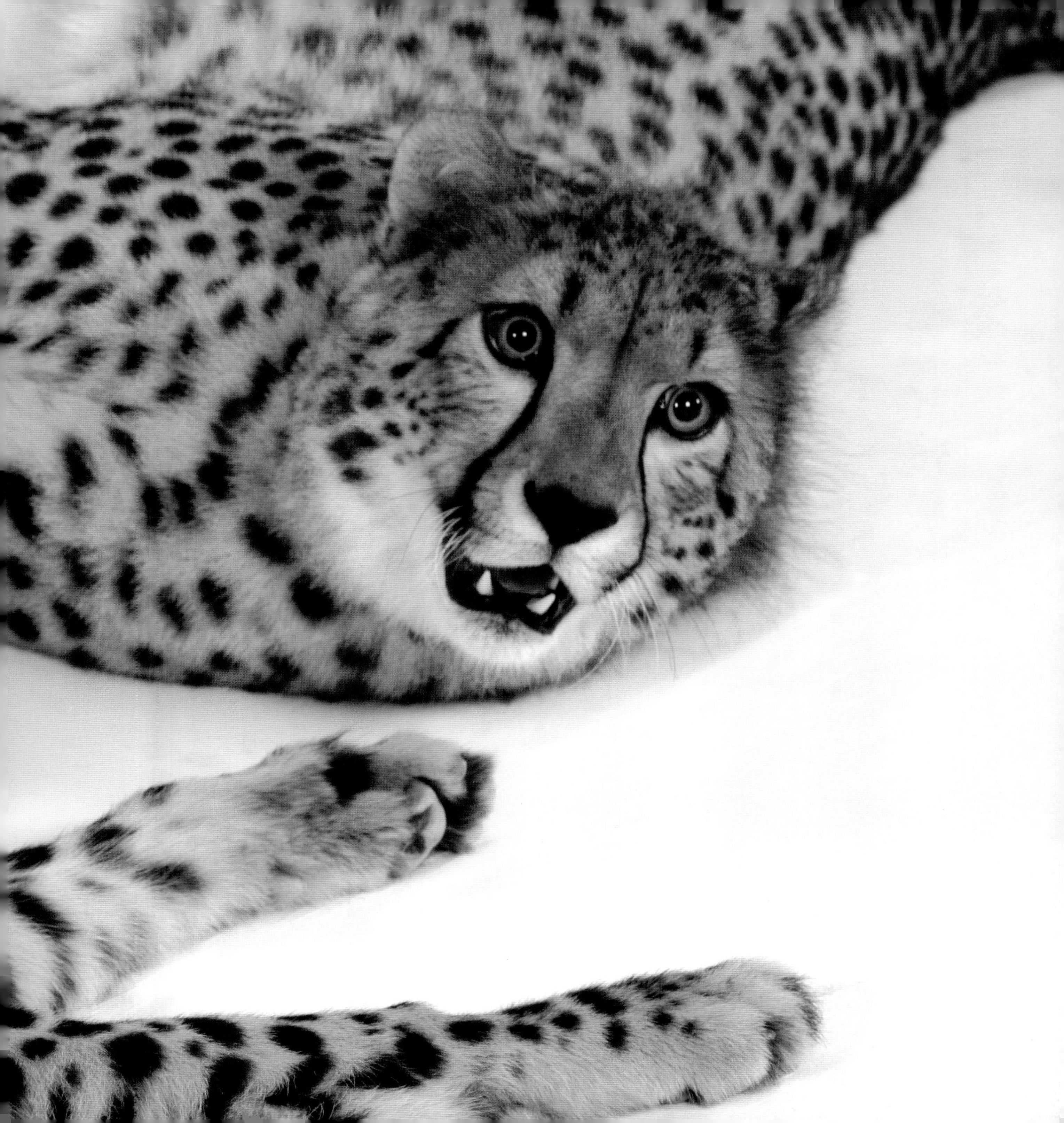

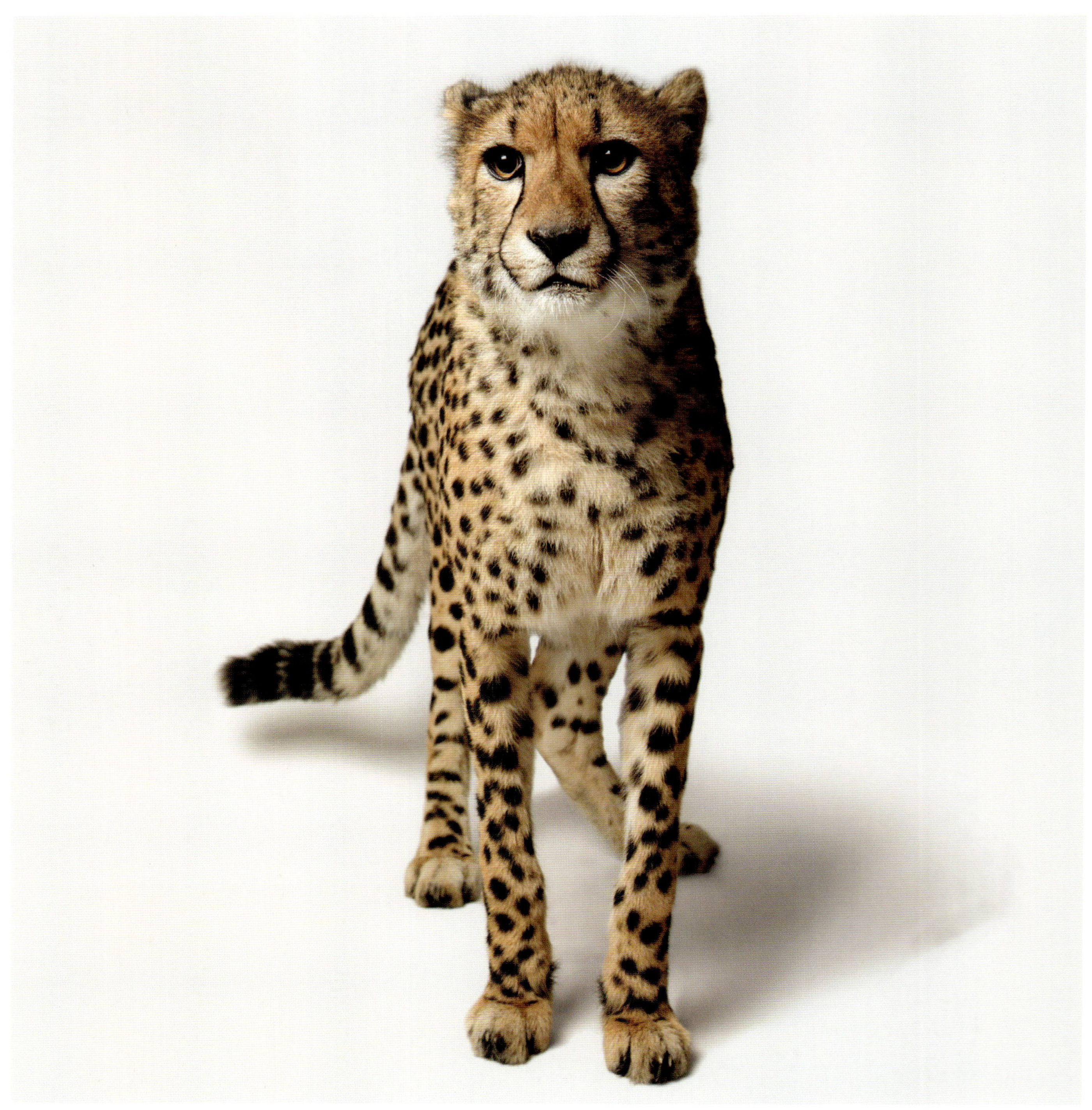

Cheetahs are associated with royalty and elegance. Princes and kings have previously kept them as pets.

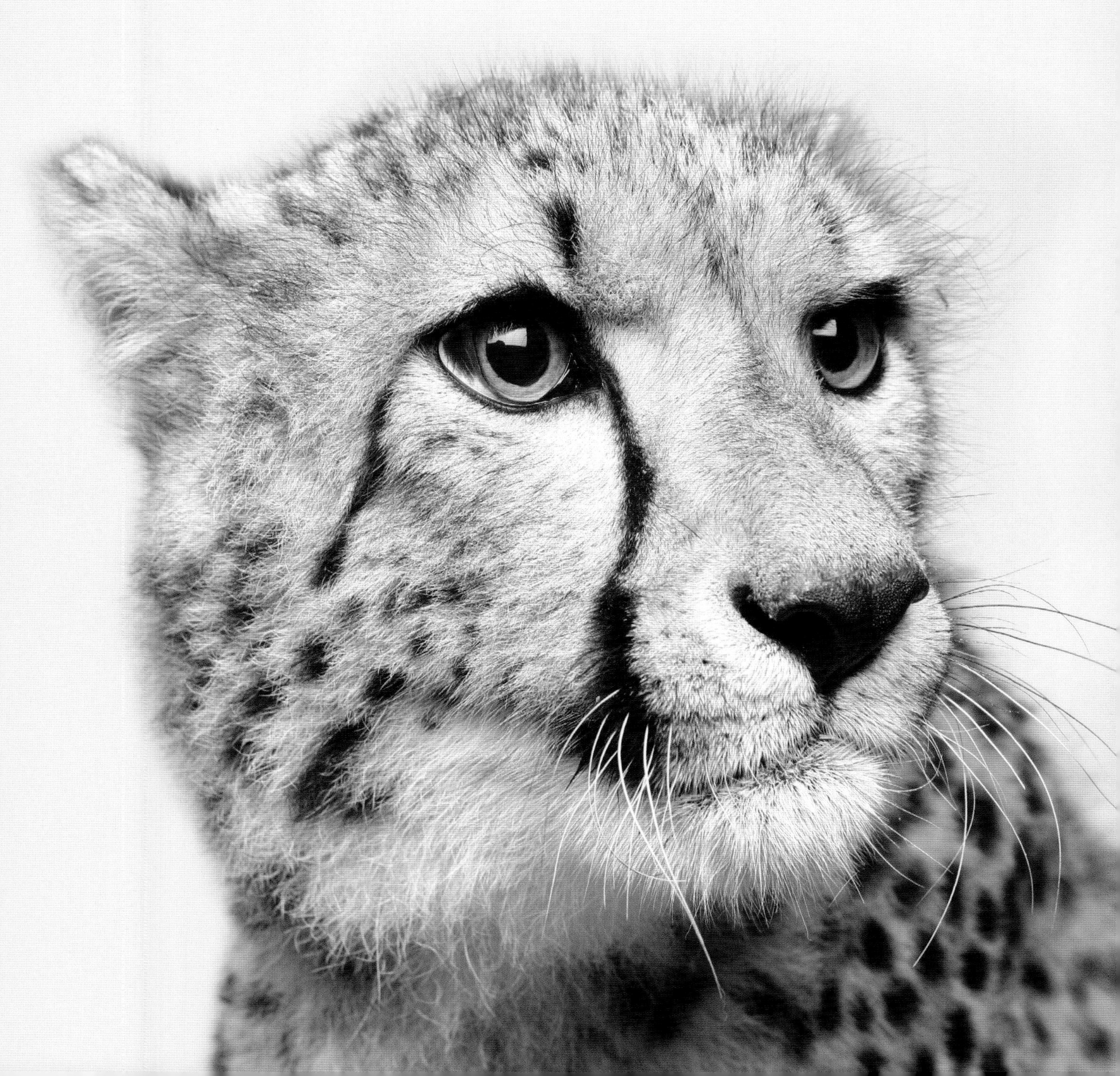

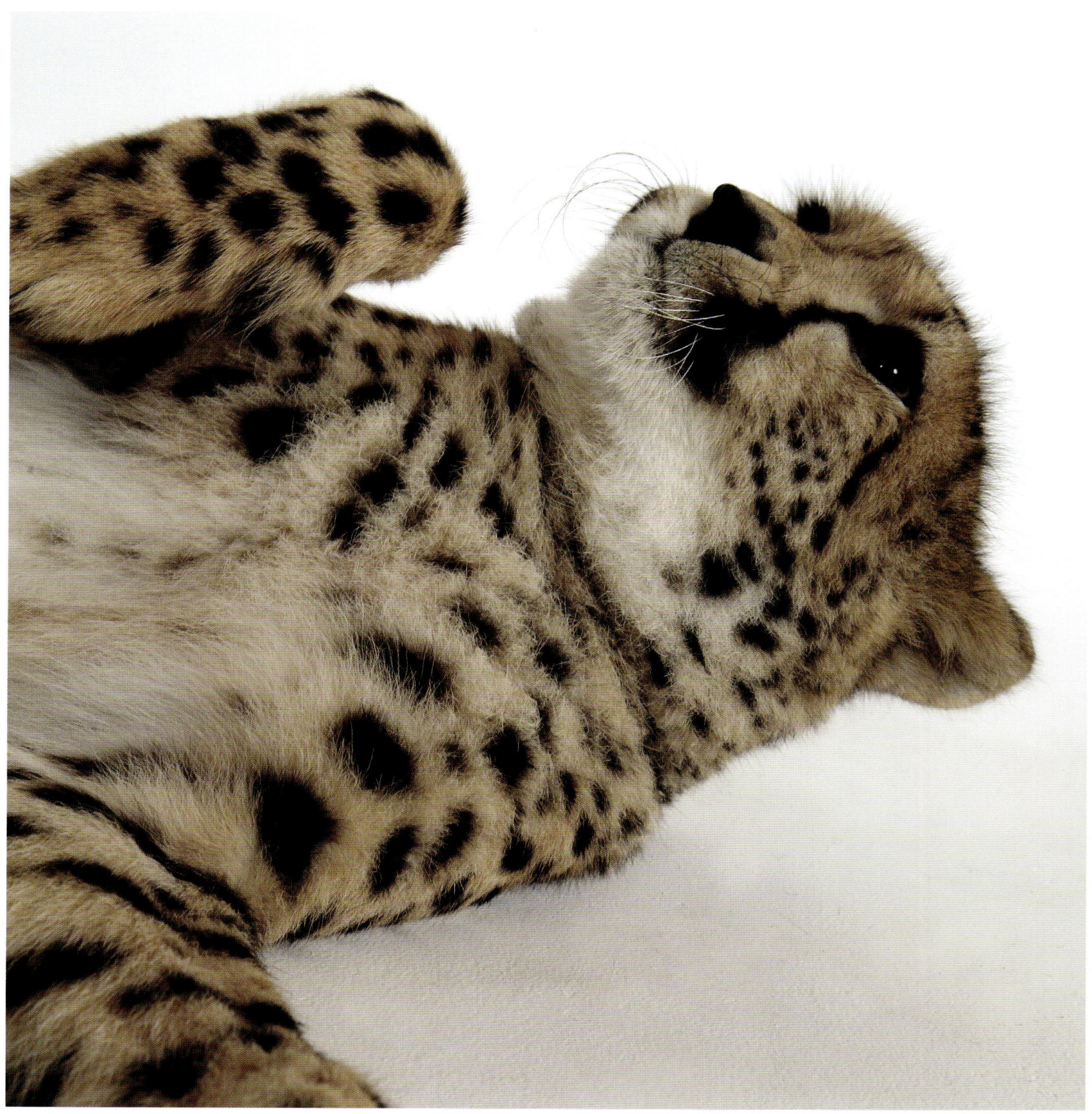

Although male cheetahs are slightly larger than females, it is difficult to tell them apart.

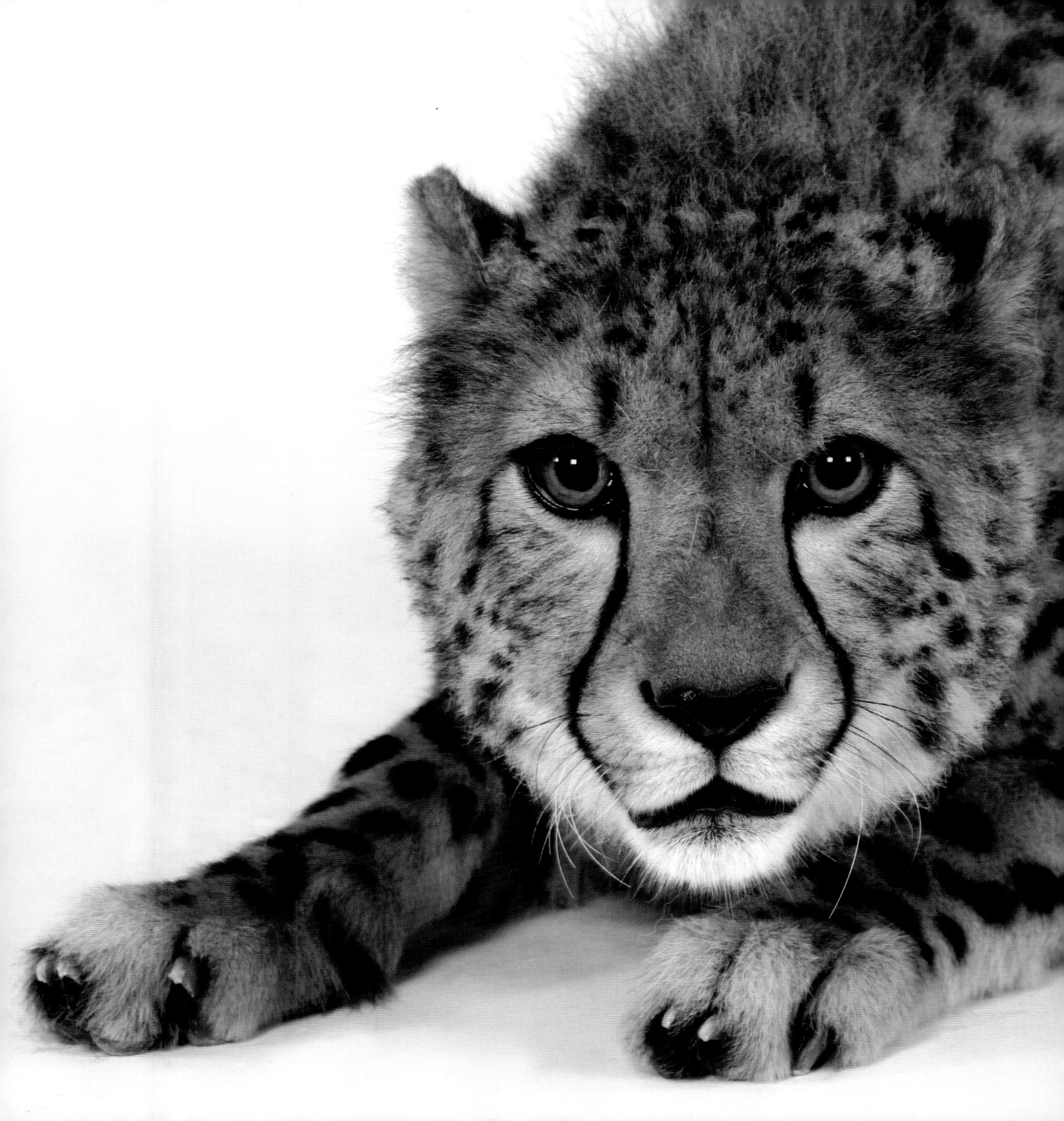

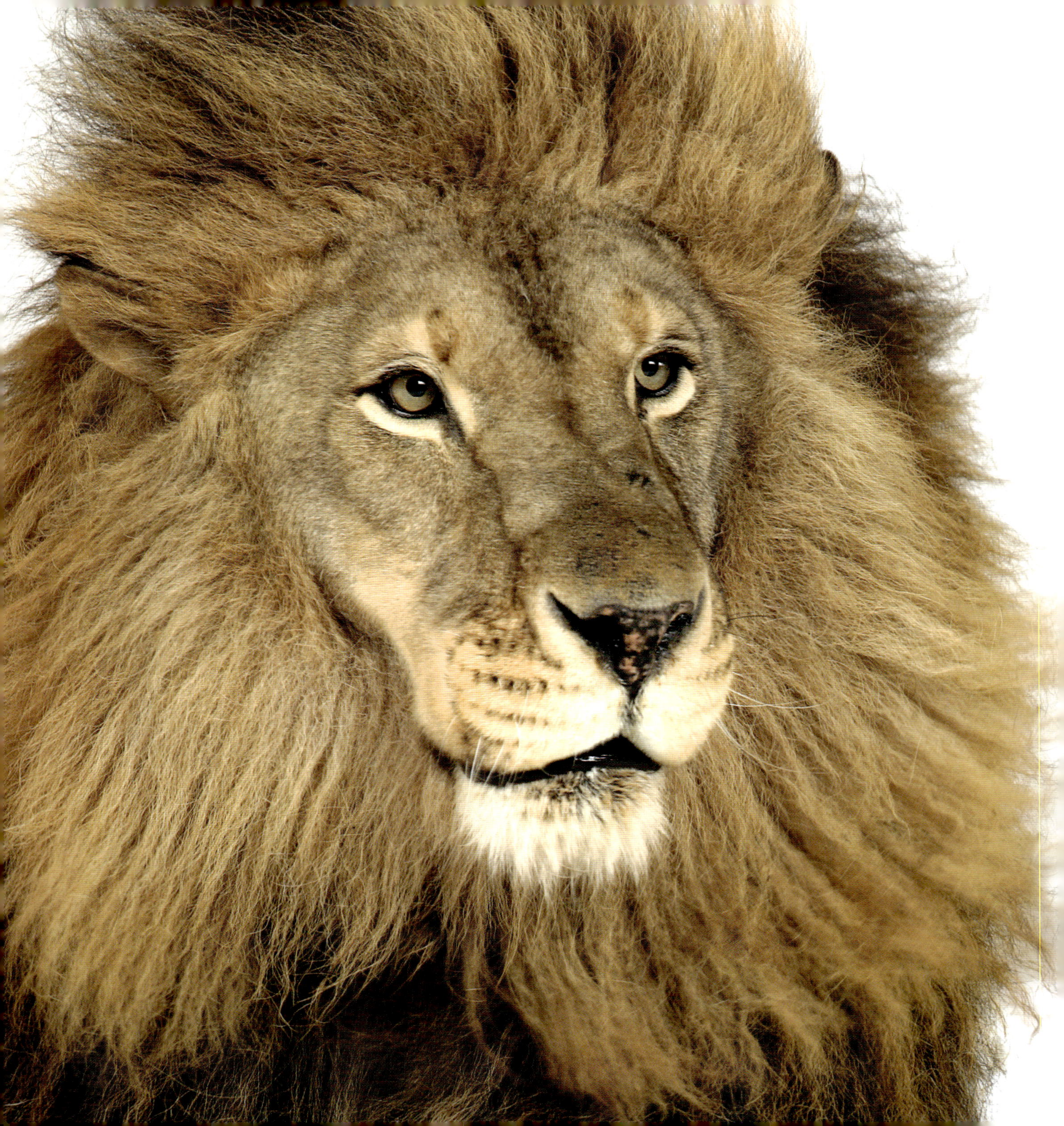

LION

Lions typically inhabit the savanna and grasslands of sub-Saharan Africa, although they can also be found in the more forested and wooded areas of this vast continent. Most lion populations are confined to large national parks and reserves such as the Masai Mara in Kenya and Kruger in South Africa. With a worldwide population estimated to be as high as 50,000, the lion is considered vulnerable but not endangered. However, a sub-species known as Asiatic lions are critically endangered with a population of just 350 in India. Male lions can grow up to 10ft (3m) from head to tail and weigh up to 550lb (250kg) and are the second largest of the big cats behind the tiger. Unusually social for big cats, they live in groups of seven to ten that contain one dominant male and are known as prides. Hunting as organized teams, the responsibility for catching prey falls to the females of the pride. Lions are voracious predators, consuming up to 66lb (30kg) of meat in one sitting.

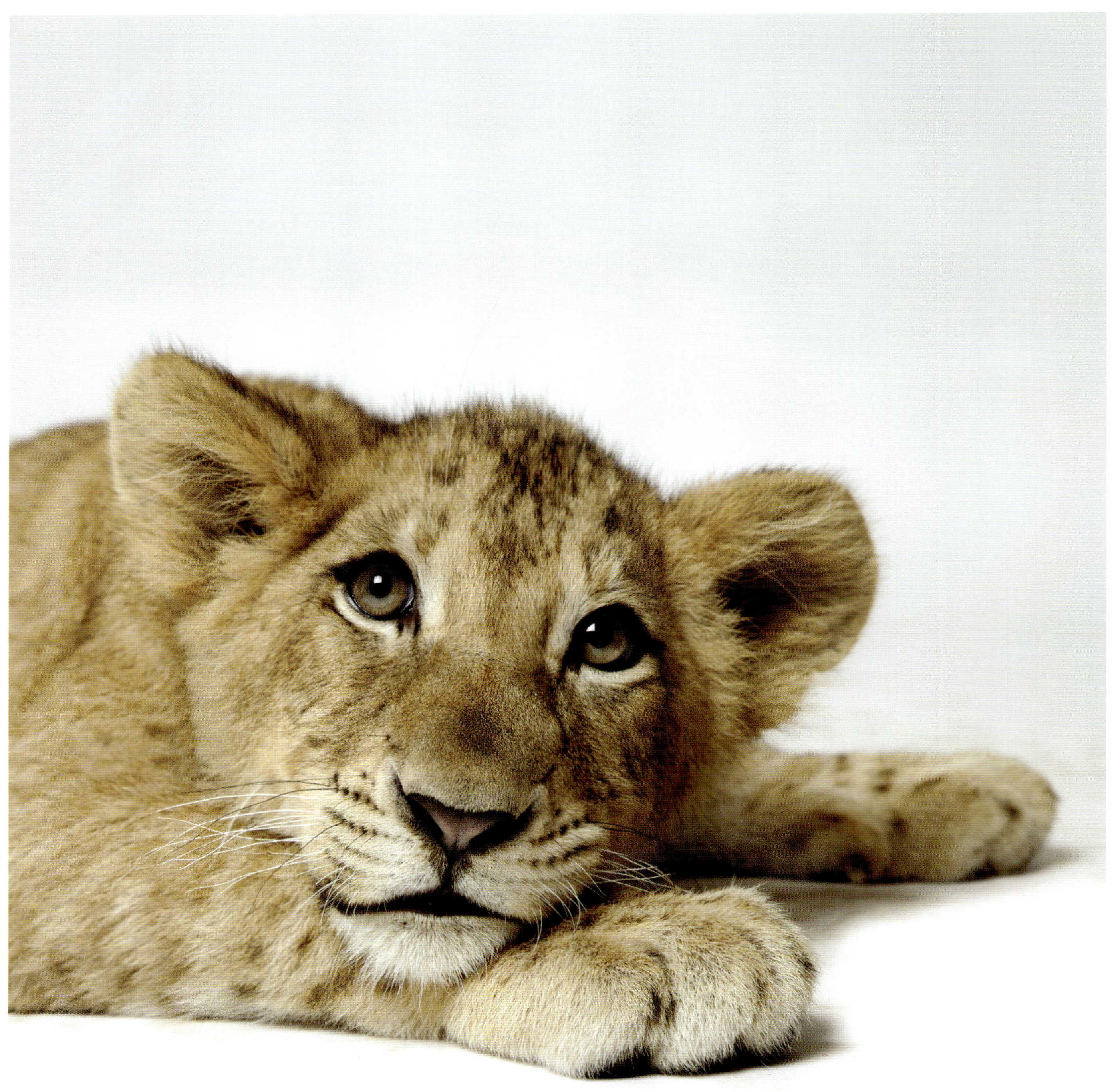

When introduced to the pride, cubs initially lack confidence when confronted with adult lions other than their mother.

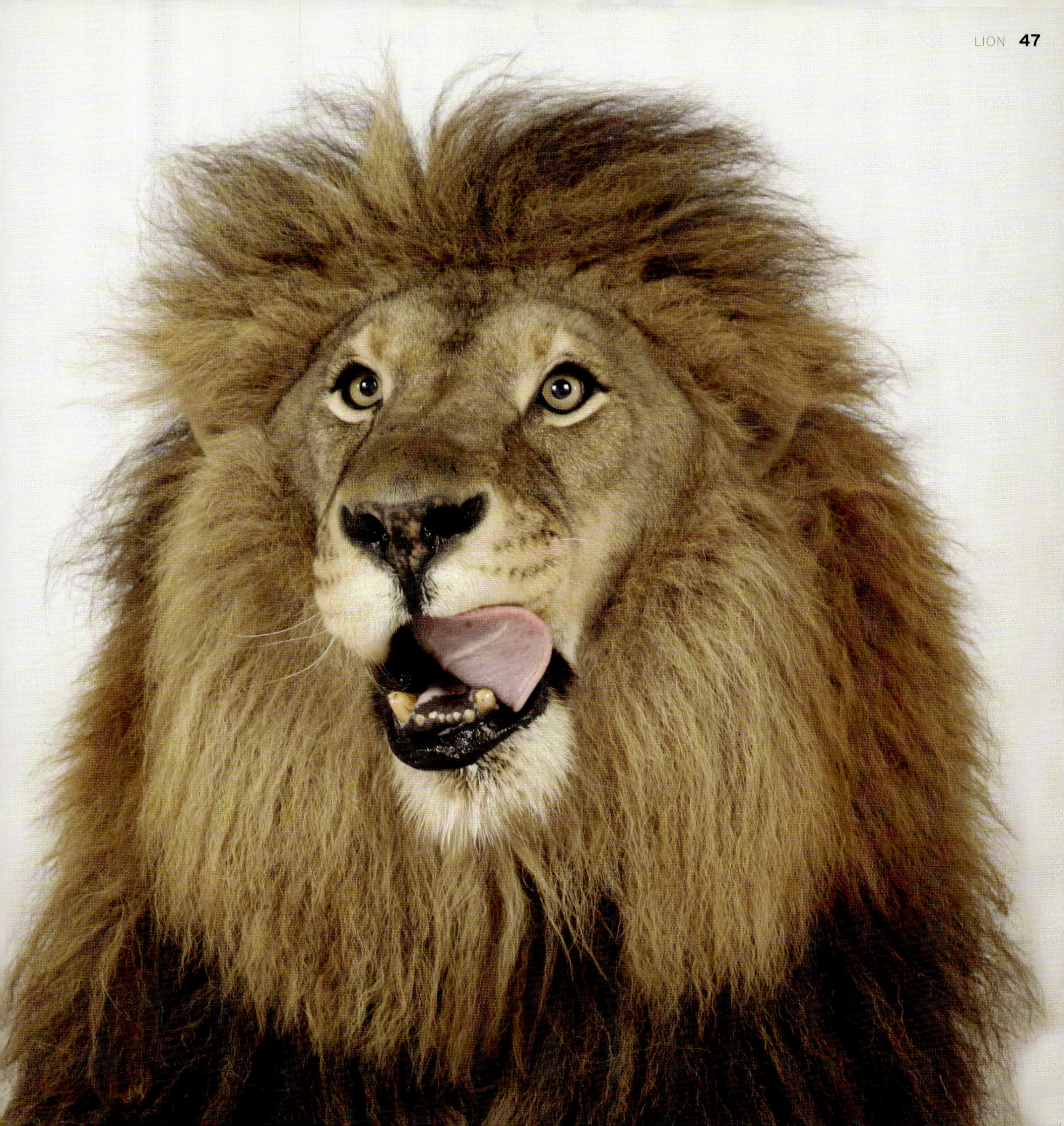

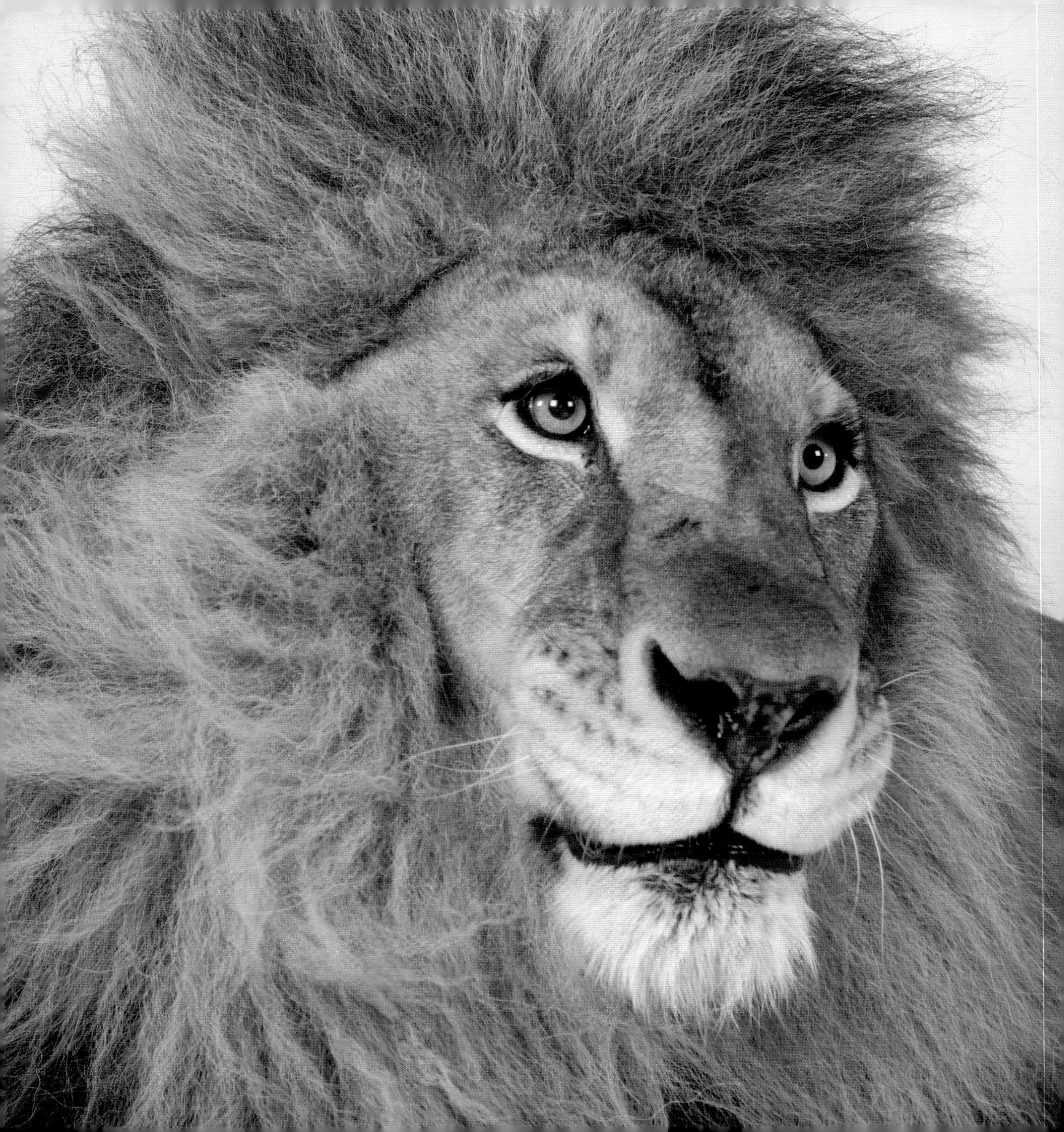

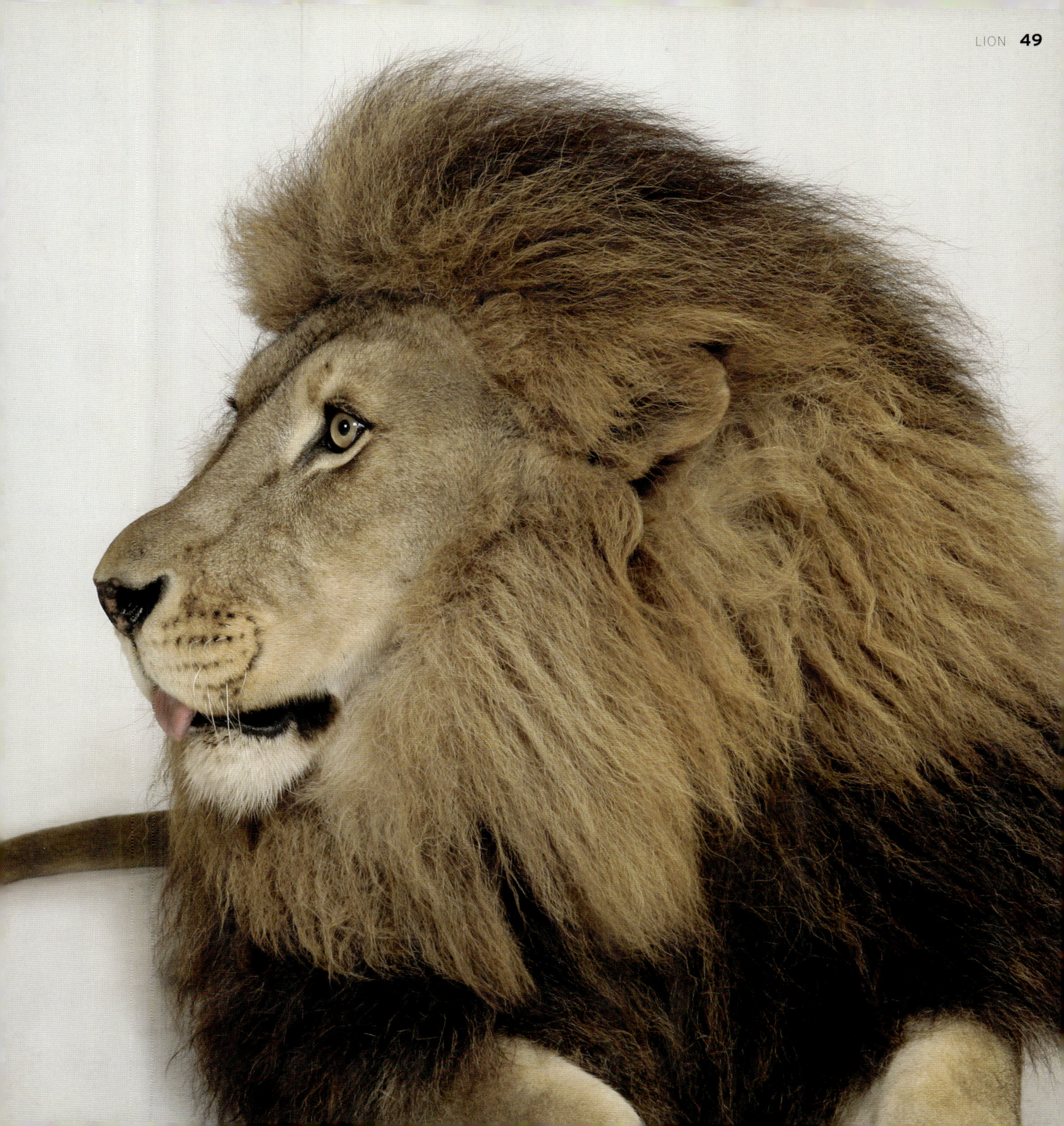

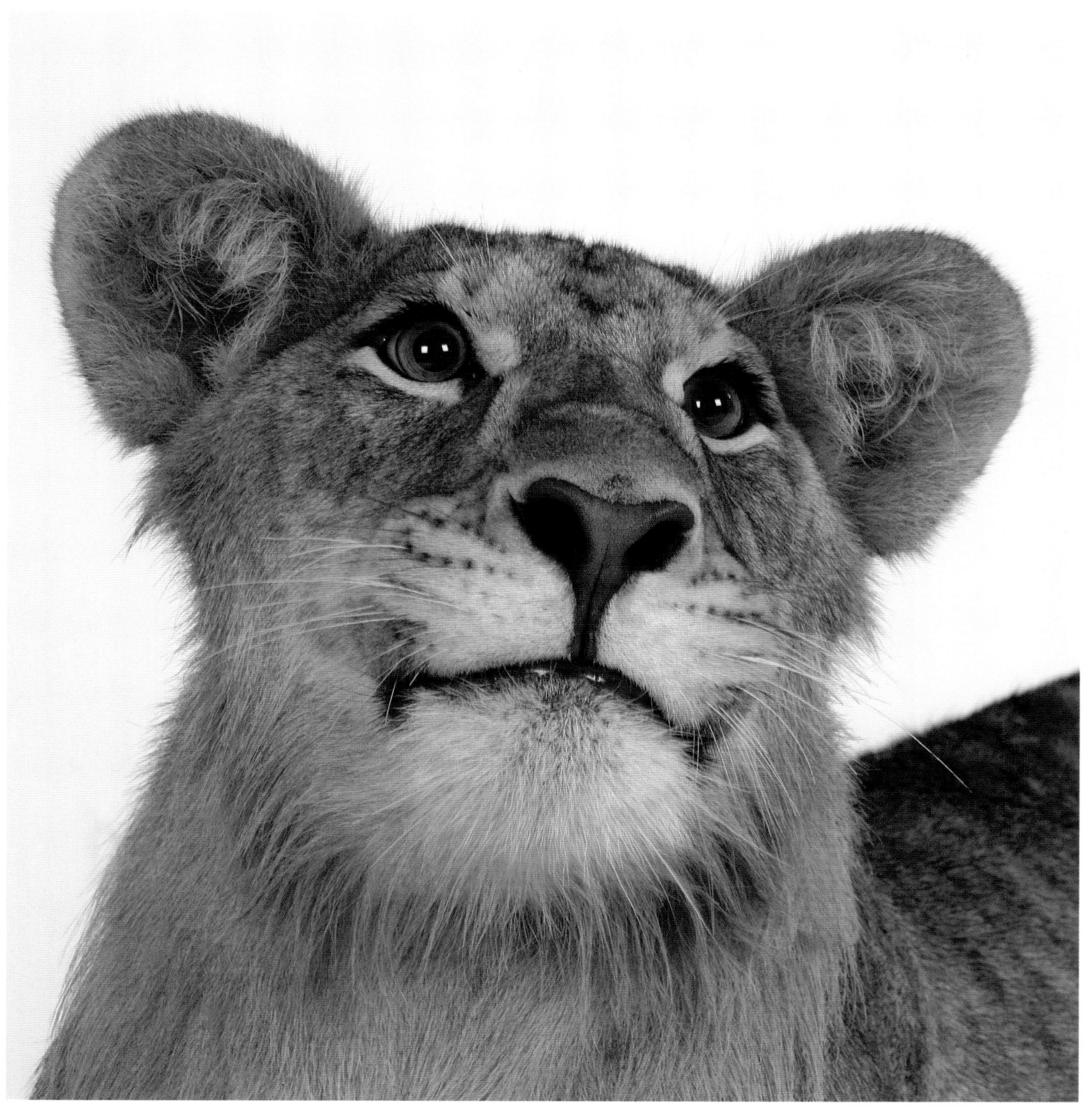

Lions have an array of facial expressions and body postures that serve as visual gestures to others in the pride.

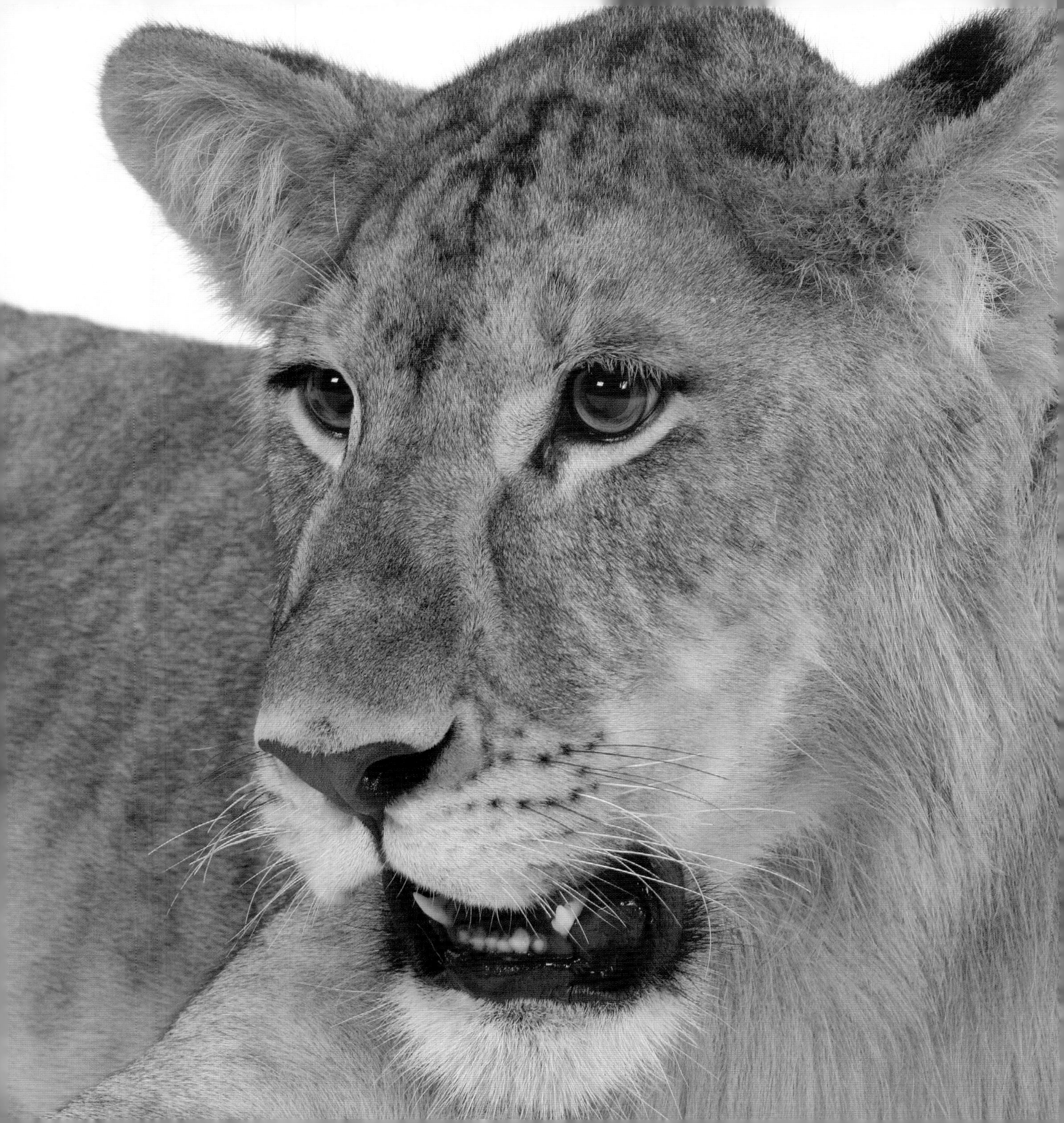

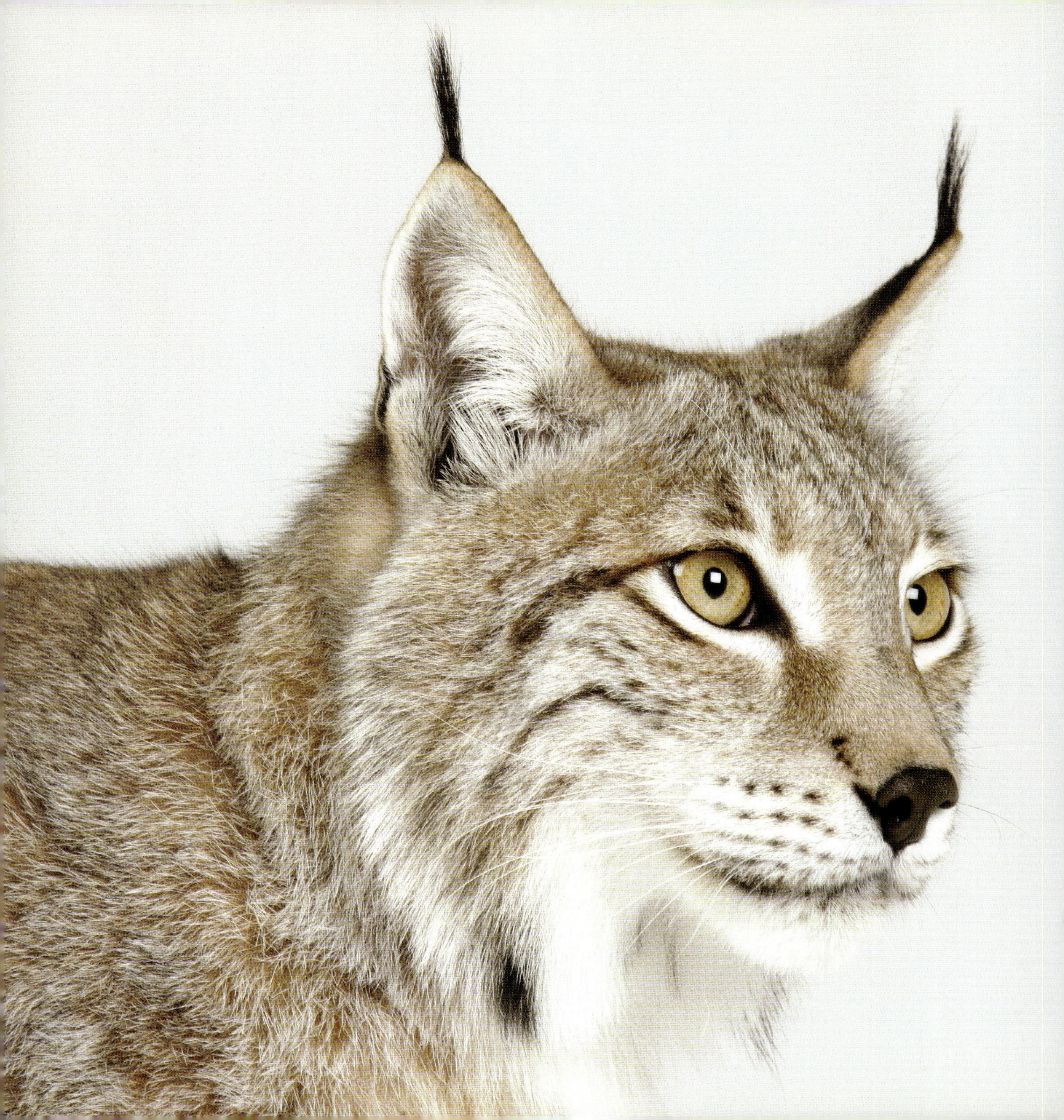

LYNX

The sturdy and adaptable lynx is found from the wilds of Alaska and Siberia to the plains of Andalucía in Spain and is not considered to be endangered. In fact an umbrella term for four types of medium-sized cat, the lynx is generally characterized by tufts of black hair on the tips of its ears and a short tail. Large whiskers and padded paws enable it to adapt to conditions ranging from mountainous rock faces to snow-covered forests. The Eurasian lynx, which is the largest of the group, can grow up to 4¼ft (1.3m) from head to tail and weigh up to 45lb (20kg). As with most big cats, the lynx is a solitary animal and prefers to do much of its hunting at night. Lynx prefer to inhabit high-altitude forested areas with lots of cover to aid them as predators, often climbing trees and, unlike most other cats, voluntarily take to the water to hunt for fish.

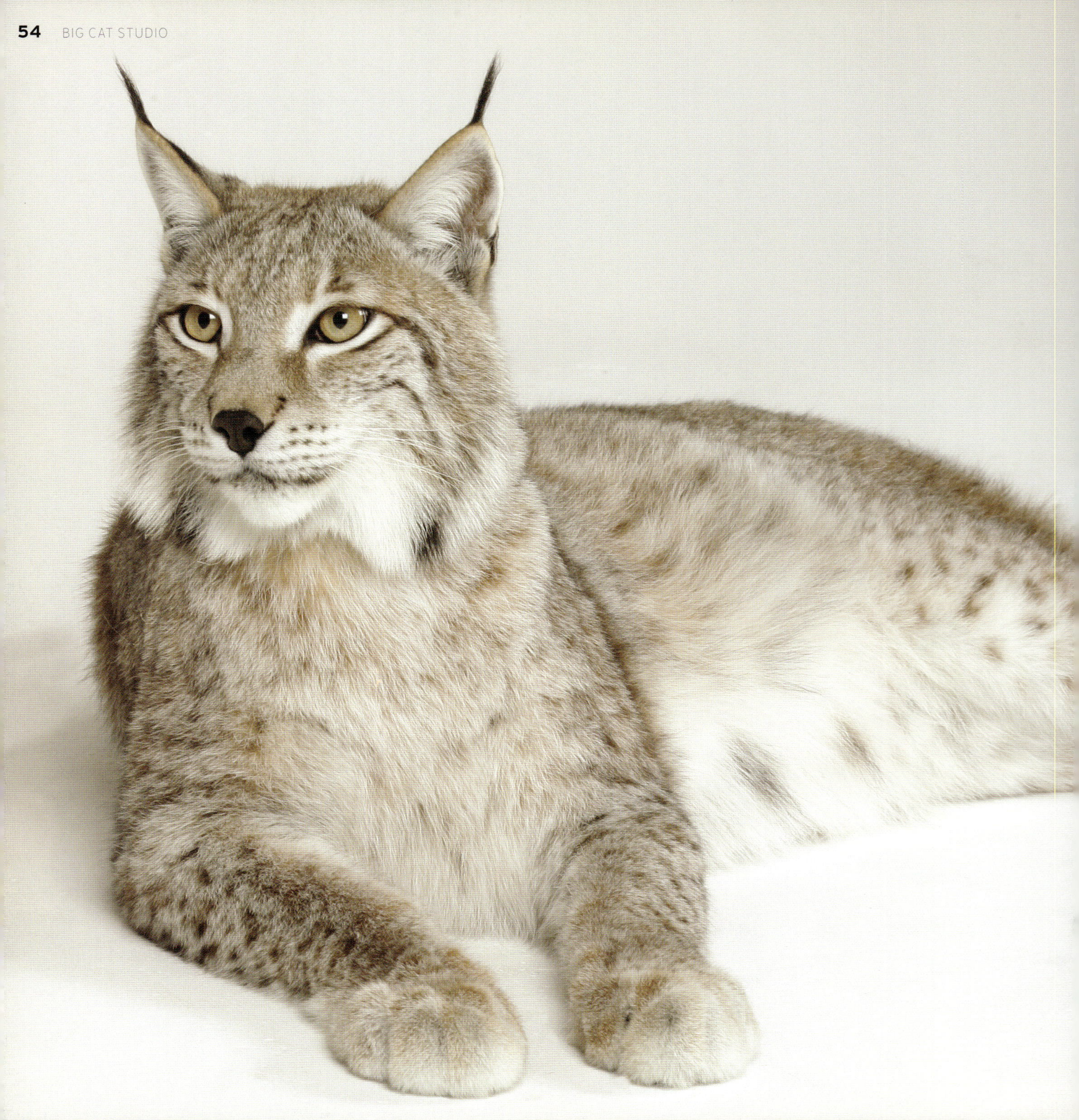

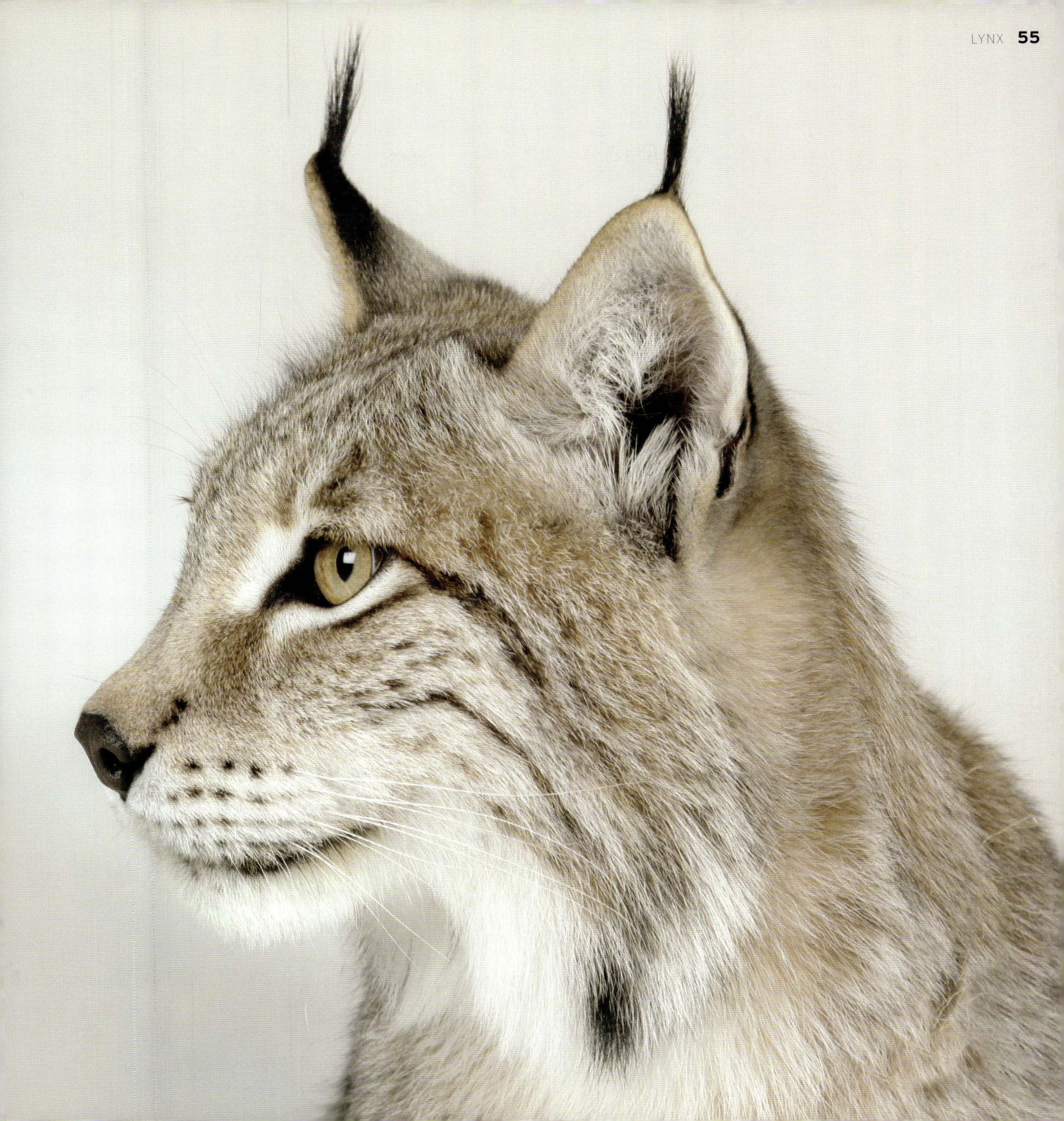

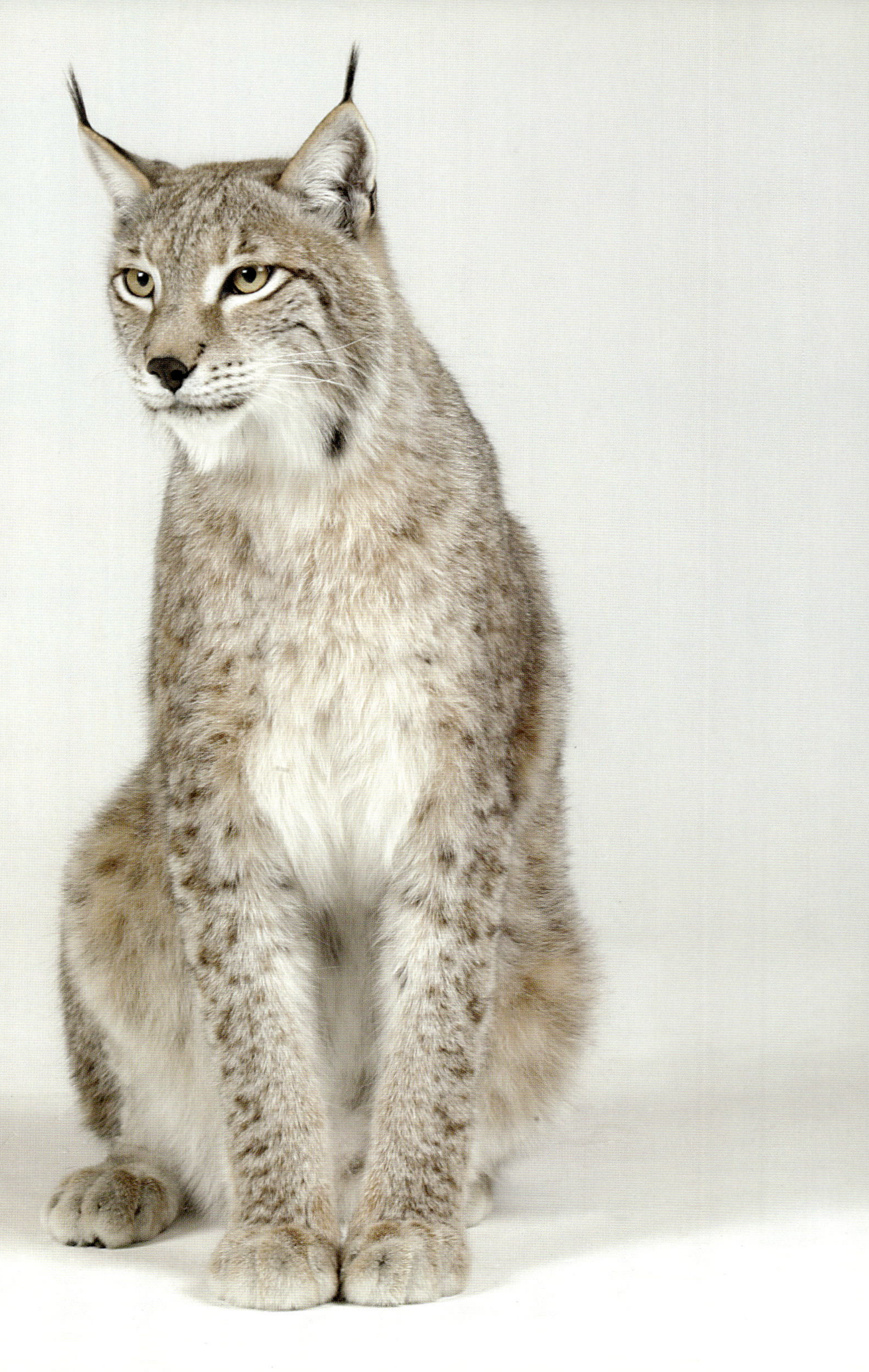

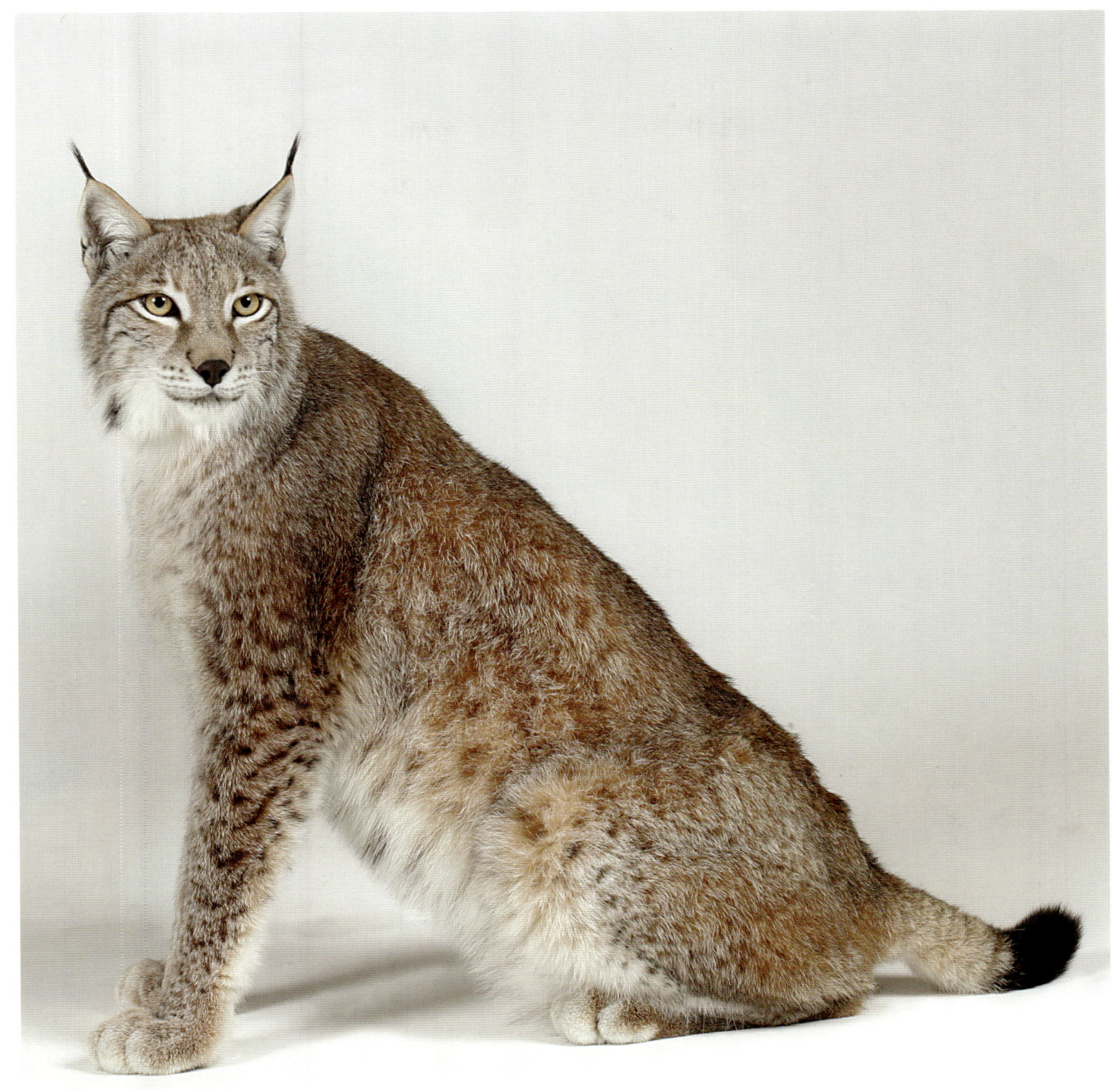

In the wild, lynx feed on a wide range of prey such as small deer, fish, birds and rabbits.

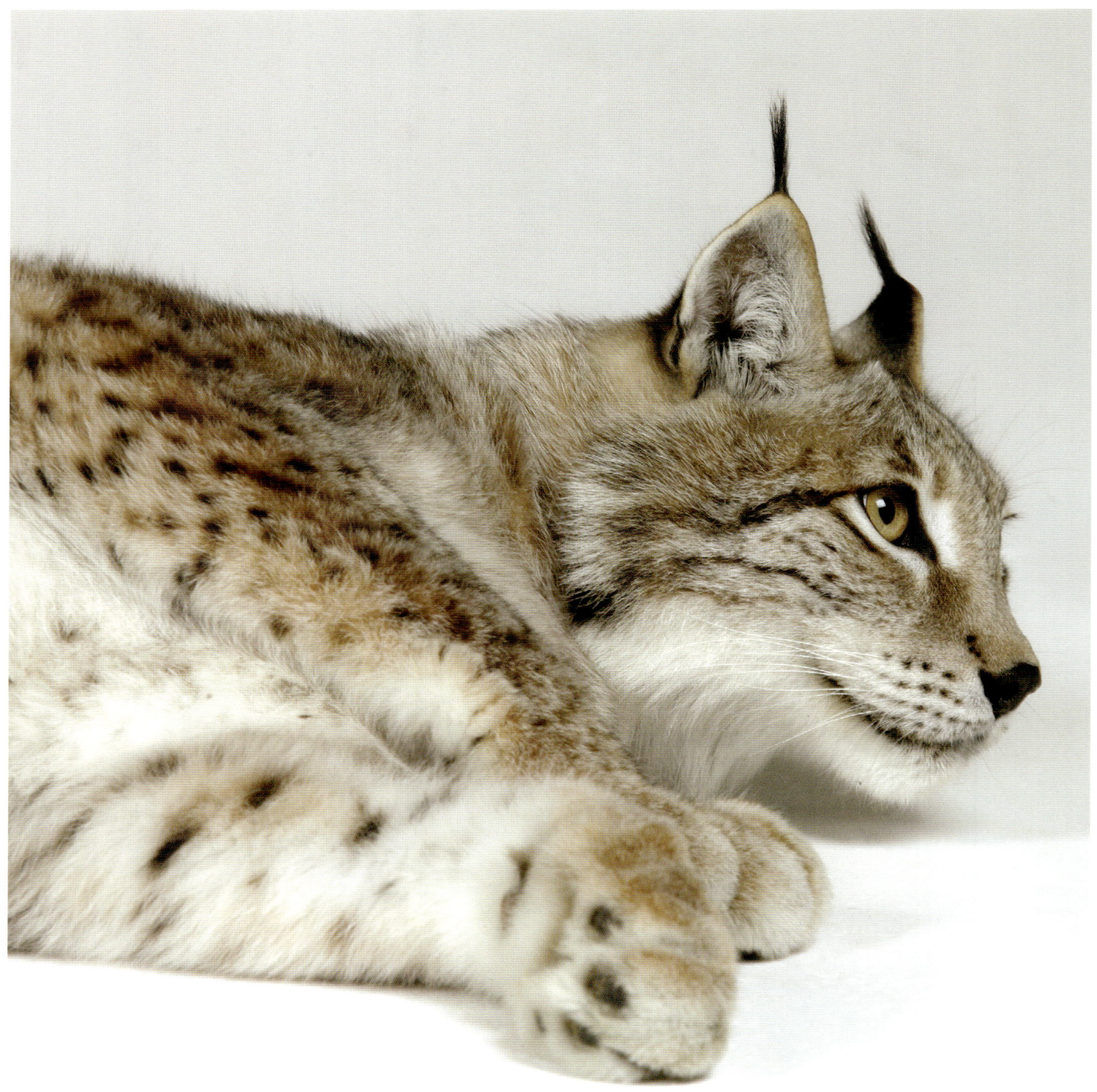

The colder the climate that lynx inhabit, the thicker and lighter their fur to give warmth and camouflage.

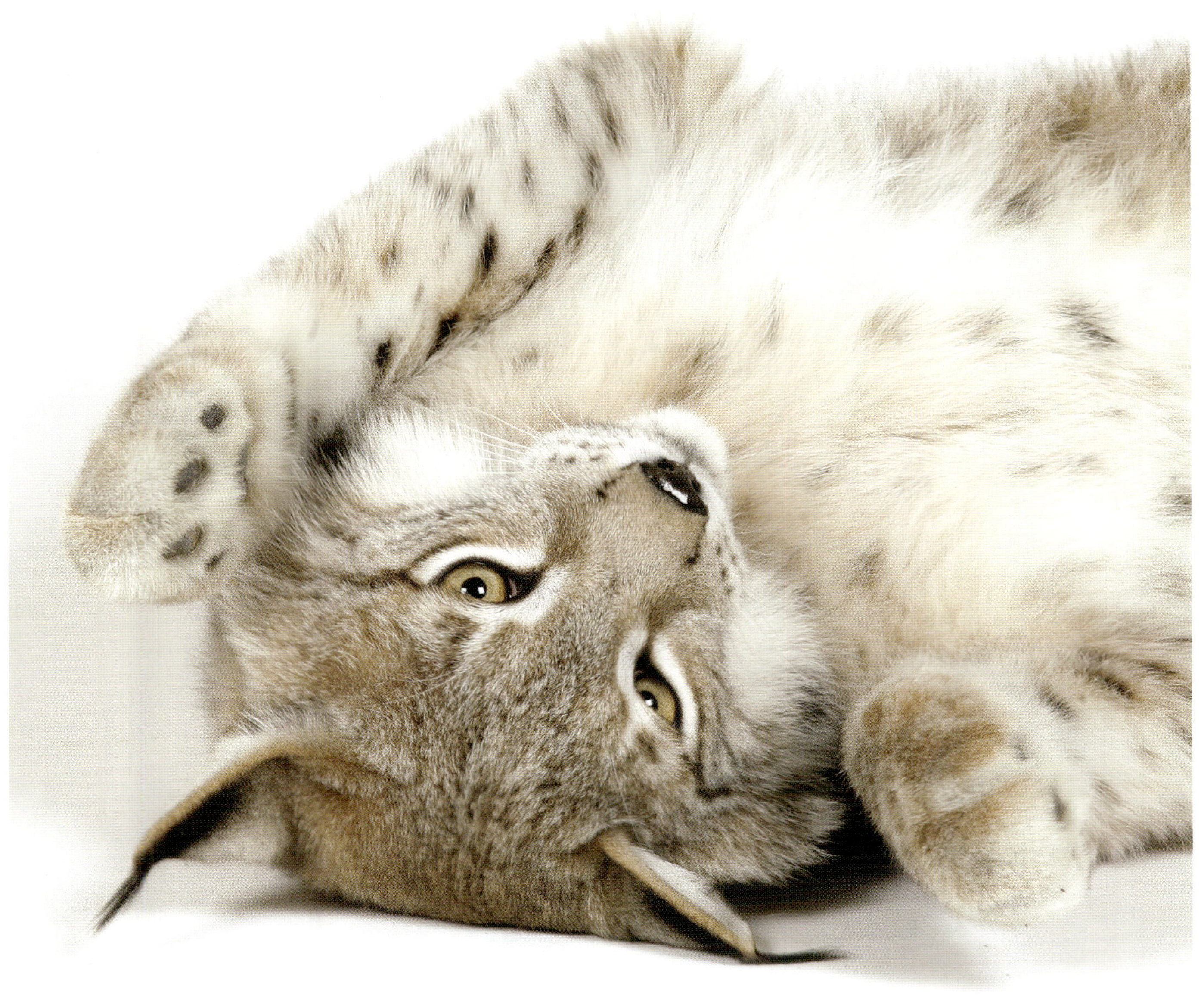

There have been numerous re-introduction schemes of lynx across Europe including Croatia and Switzerland.

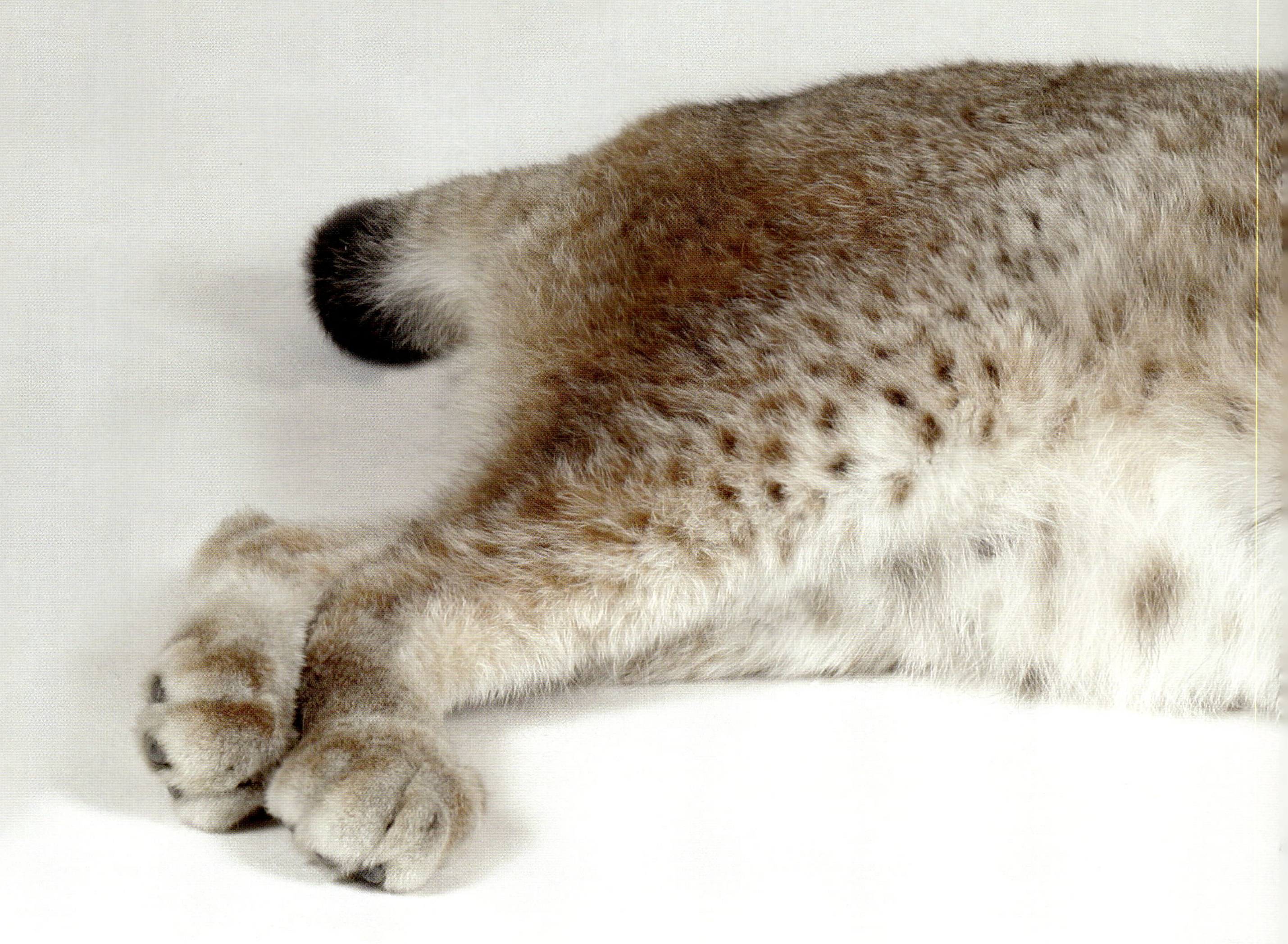

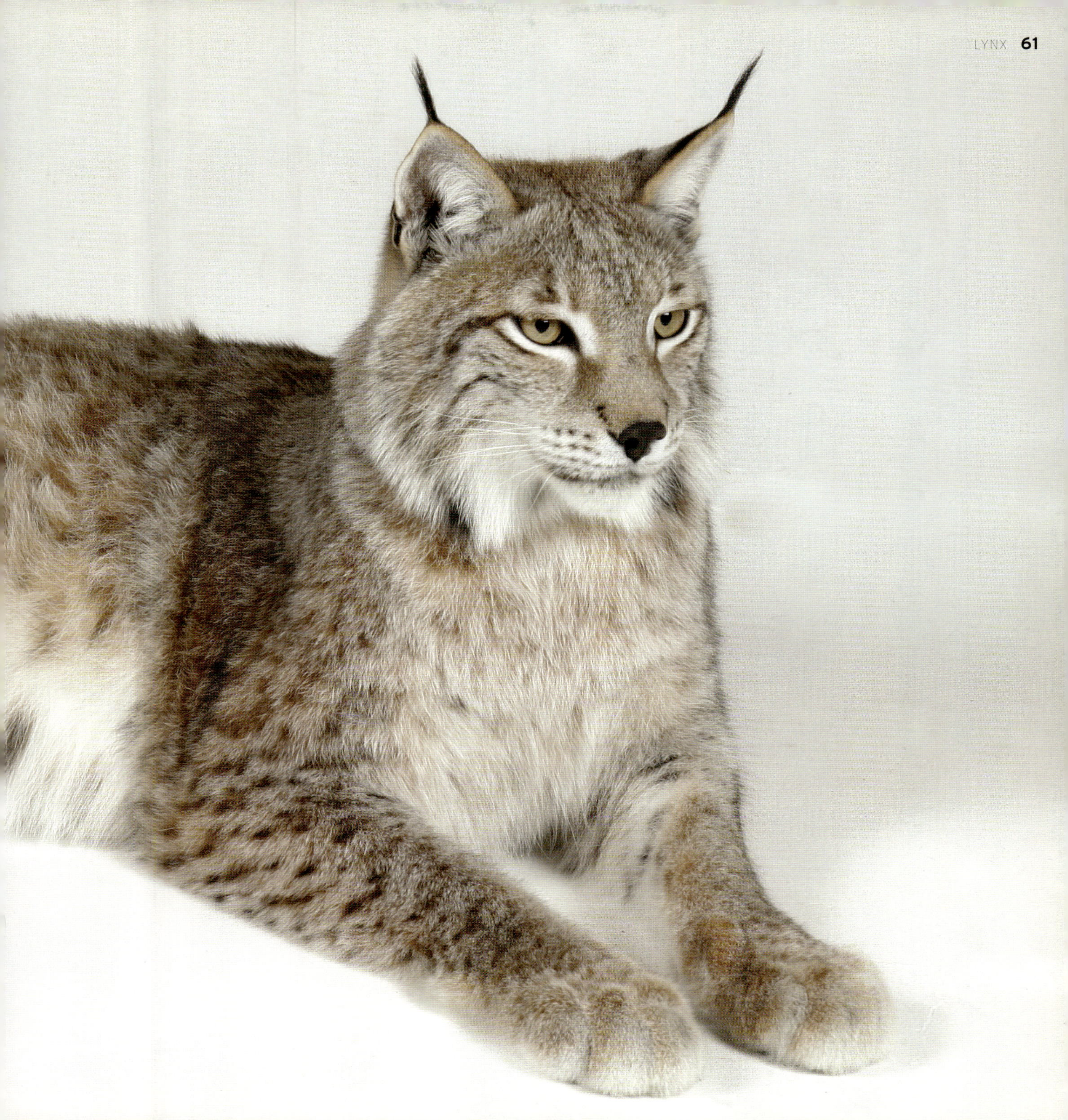

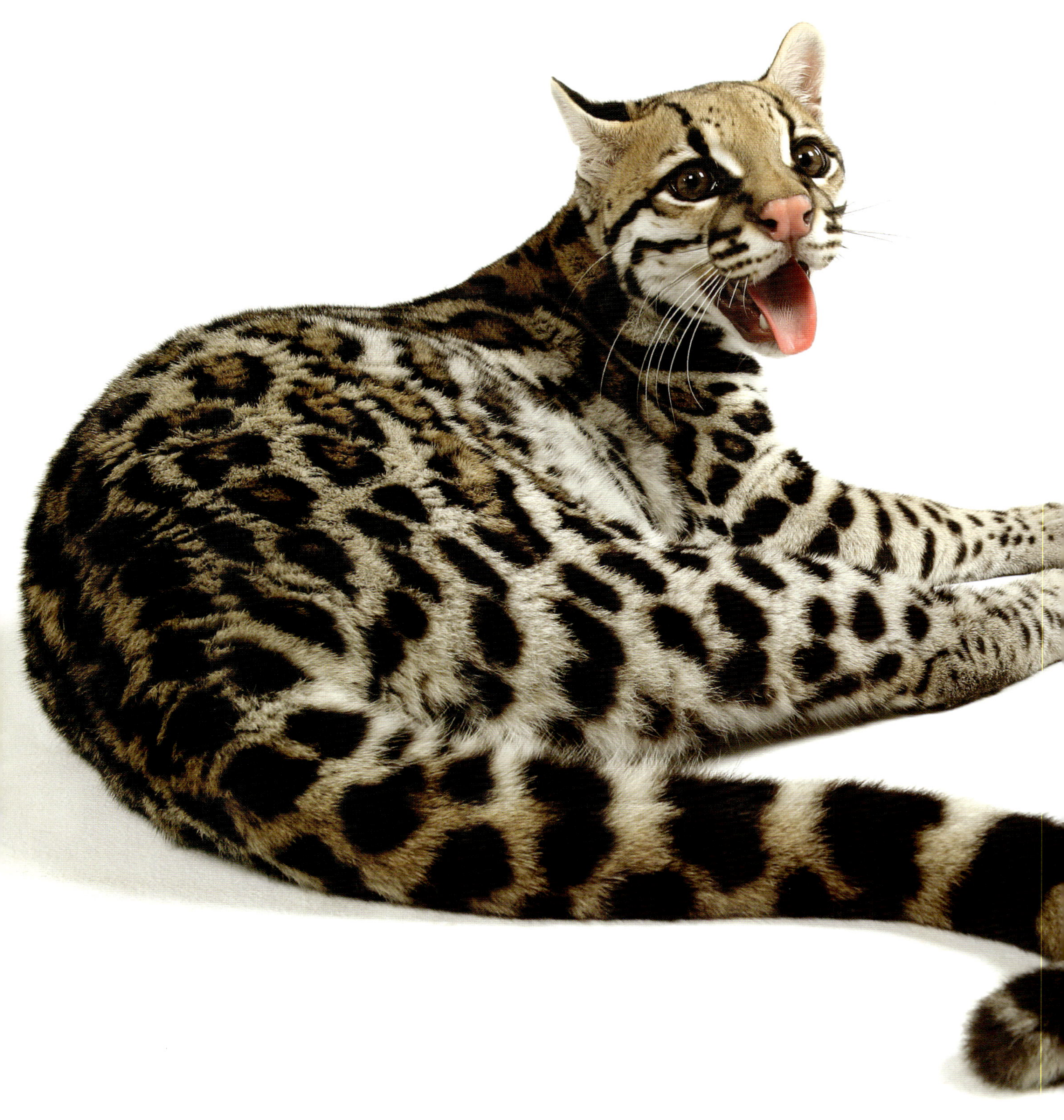

OCELOT

The nocturnal ocelot is one of the smallest of the wild cats and is distributed widely across Central America and the rainforests of South America. Classed as a vulnerable and endargered species until 1996, the ocelot's population in the wild has risen and is now of less concern to environmentalists. Resembling a domestic cat in size and shape, ocelots can grow up to 3ft (1m) from head to tail and weigh up to 30lb (14kg). Skilled hunters with excellent night vision, they prey on small rodents, reptiles and fish, but rarely attempt to kill any animal that is larger than themselves. Ocelots are solitary cats and will fight other ocelots to the death in territorial disputes. Because of their appearance and size, ocelots have long been sought after as pets. The surrealist Salvador Dali owned a pet ocelot and demand for the cat remains high in the US.

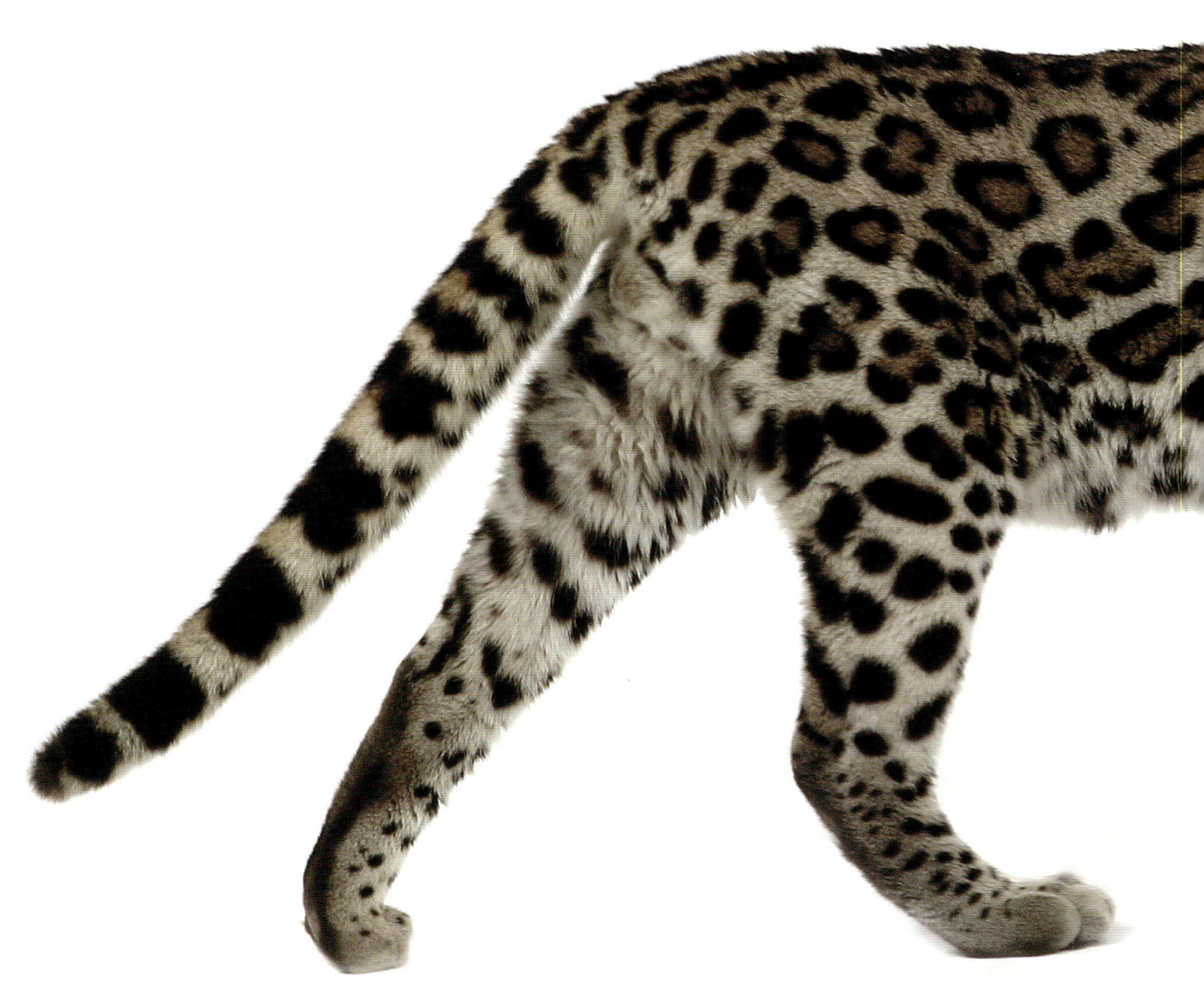

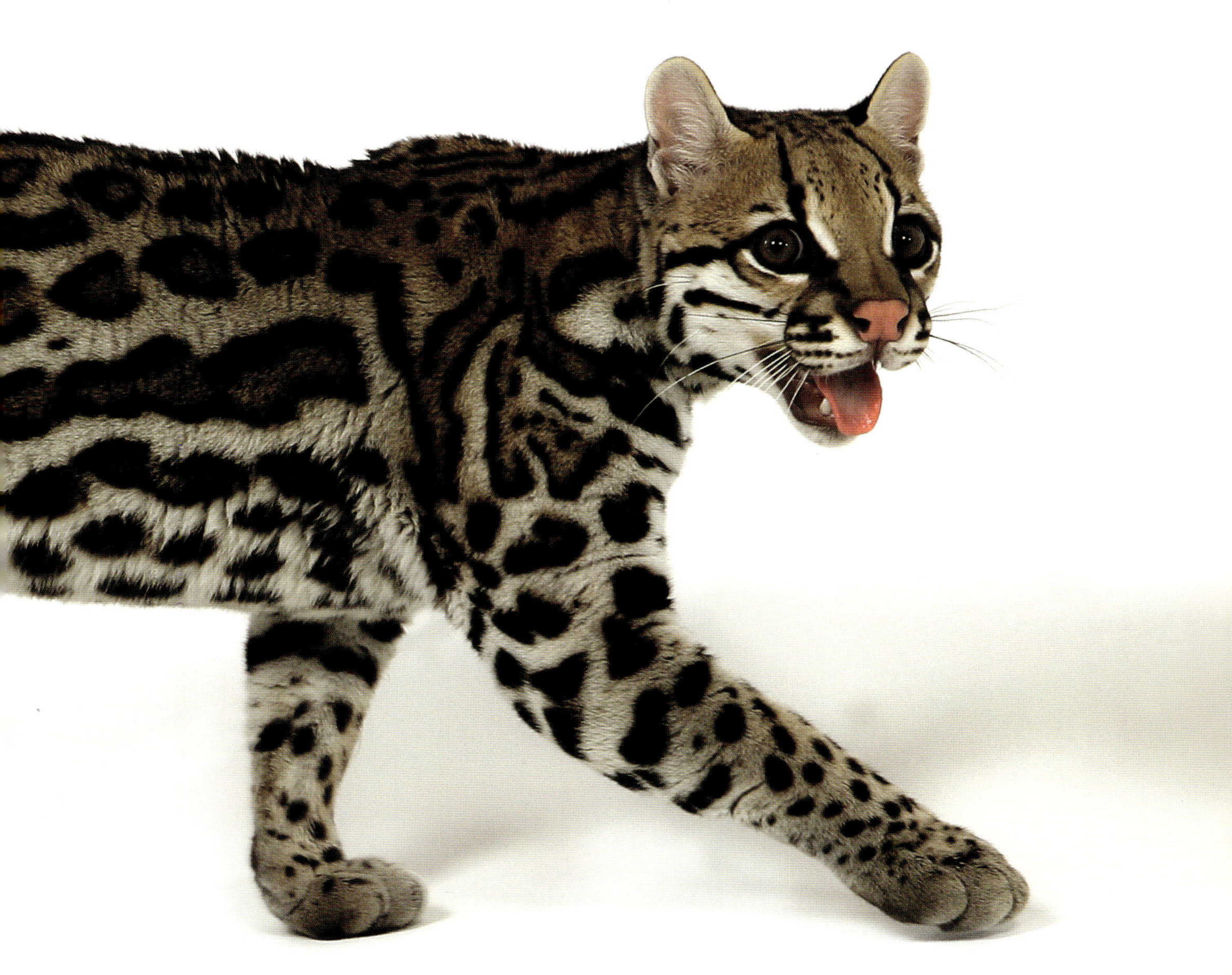

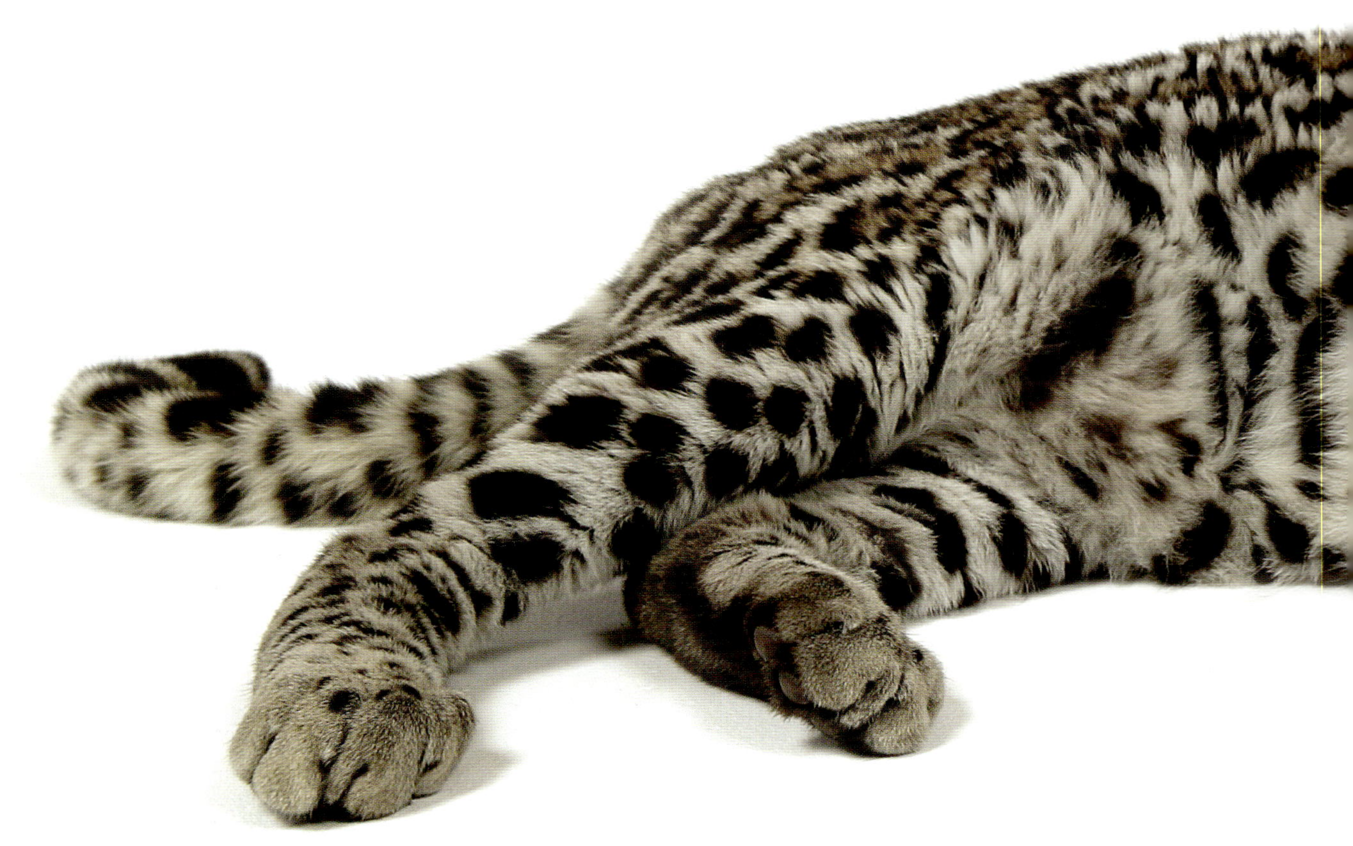

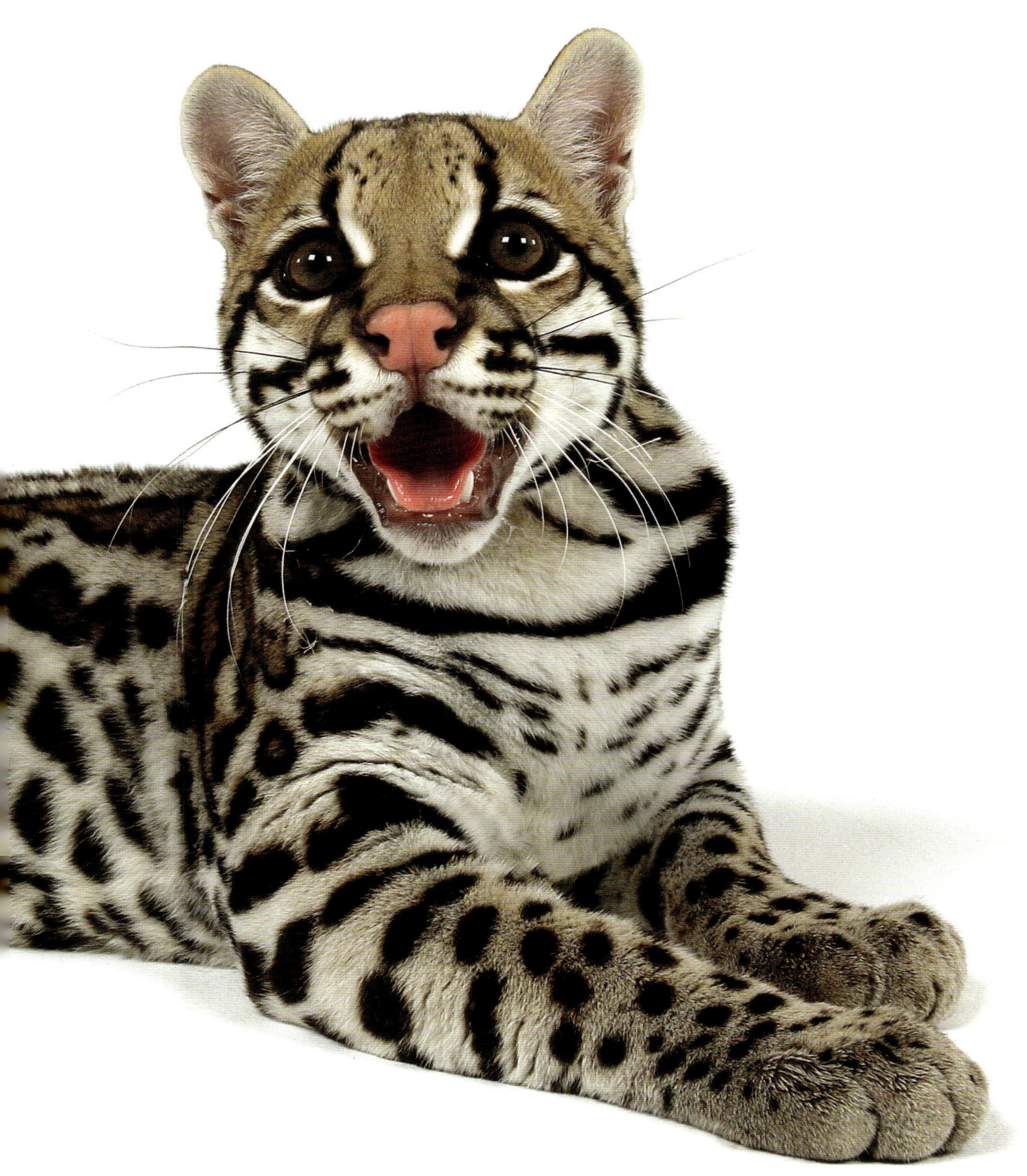

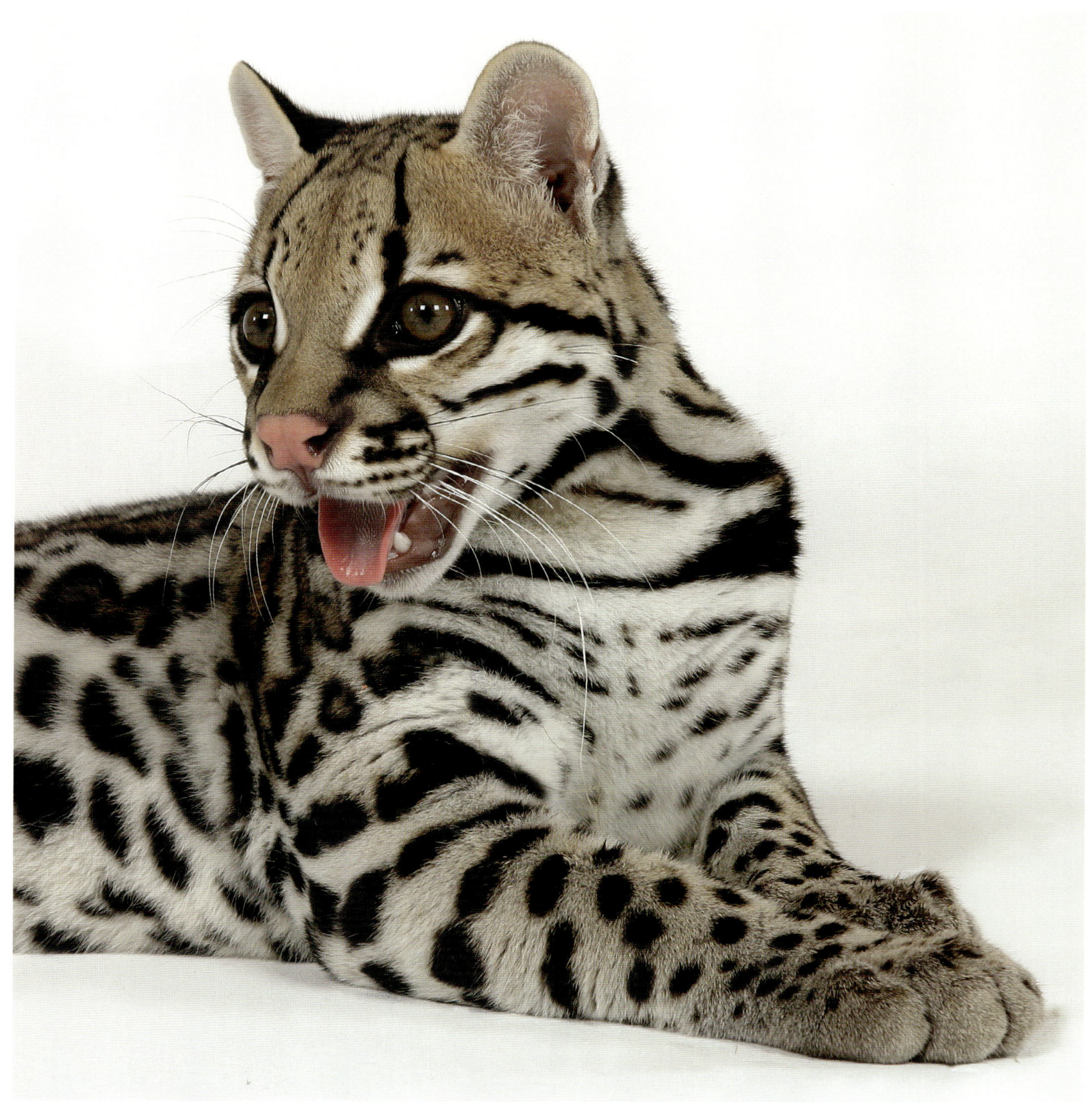

The ocelot is often hunted for its striking marbled fur and is protected in most countries where it lives.

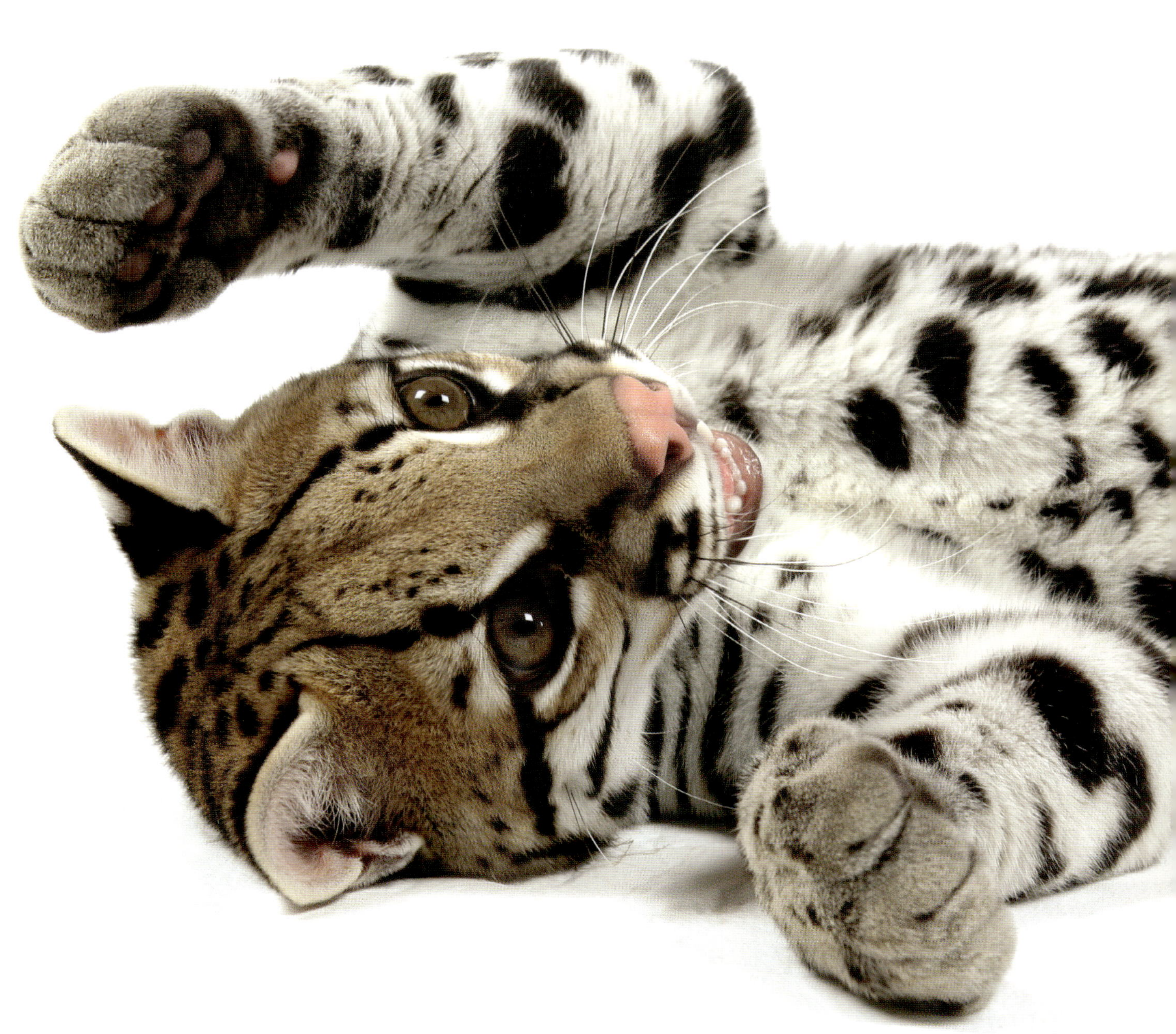

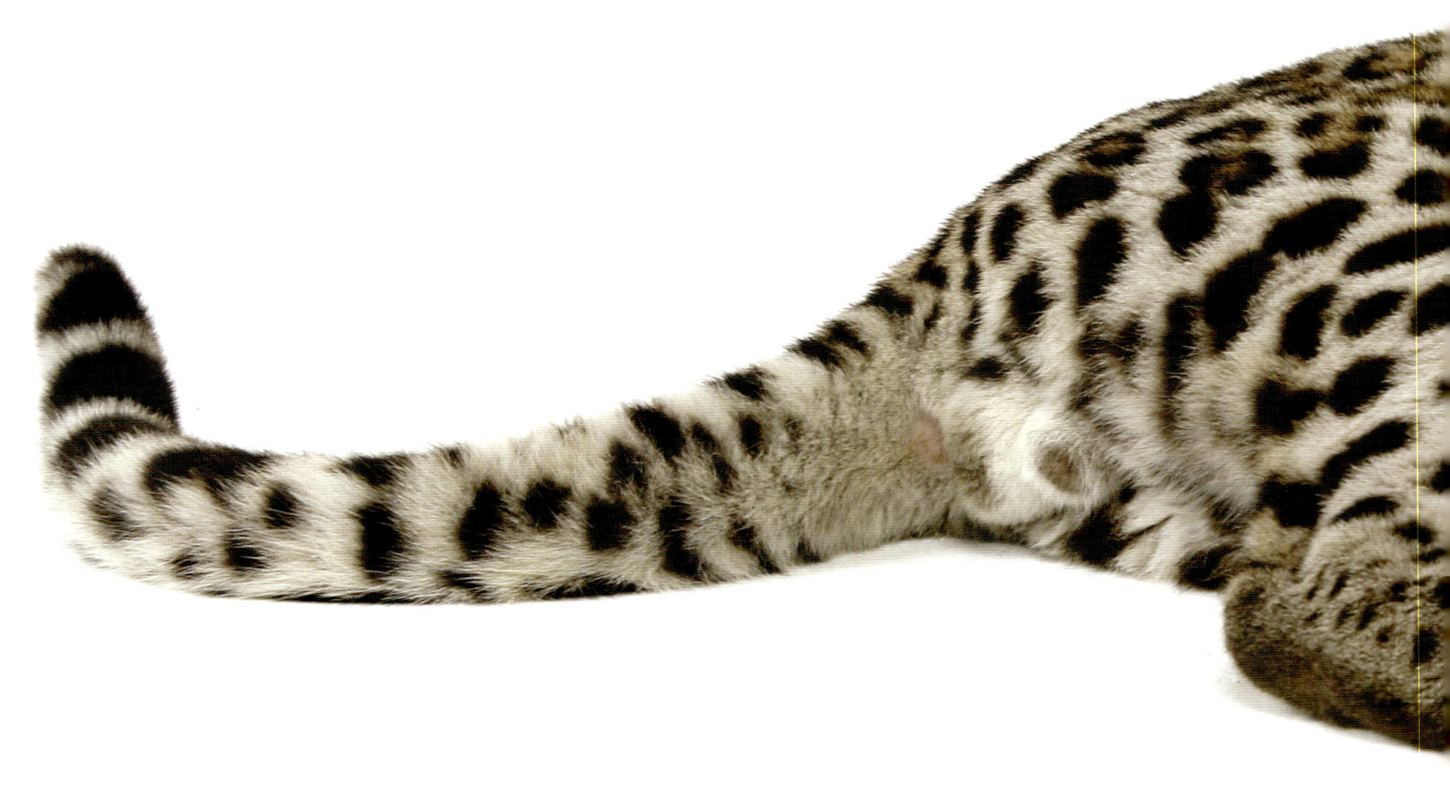

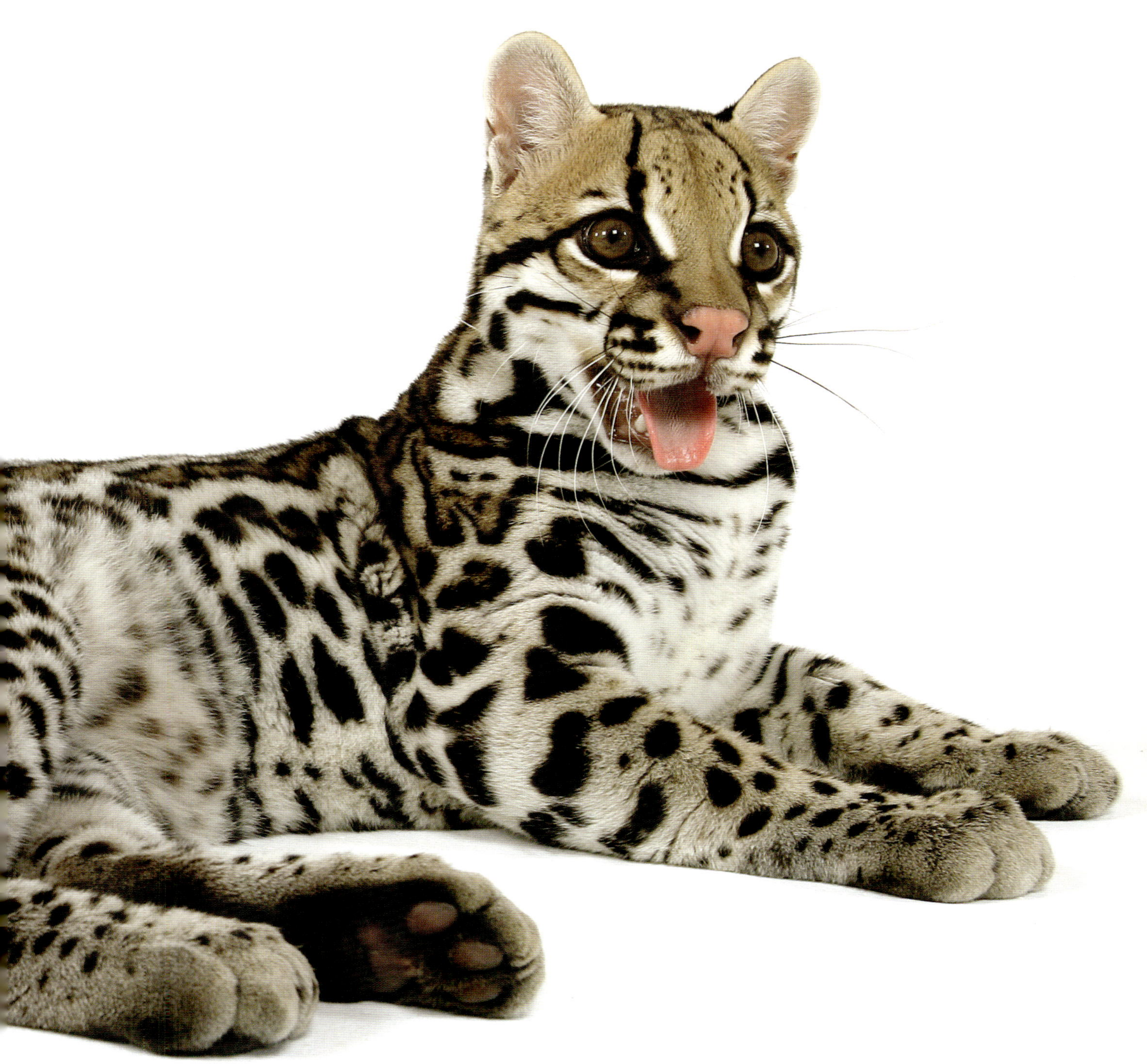

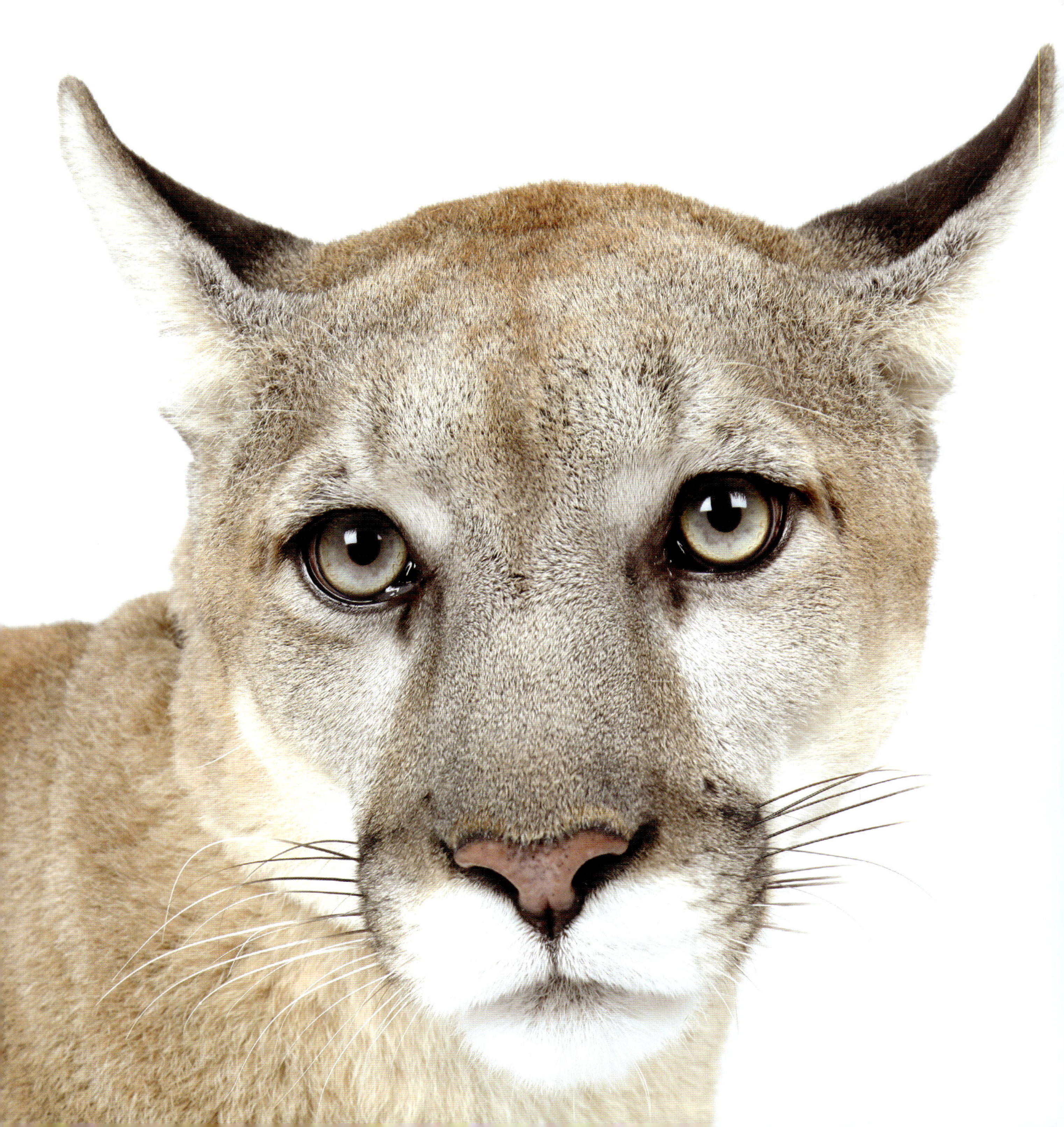

PANTHER

The panther's natural habitat extends from northern Canada to the southern Andes in South America. The panther population of North and South America is estimated to be around 50,000 and is not thought to be endangered. Panthers are the fourth heaviest big cat in the world, measuring around 8ft (2.5m) from nose to tail and weighing up to 198lb (90kg). Resembling a giant domestic cat, they are slender and extremely agile, capable of vertical leaps of up to 18ft (5.5m). Relying on their feline instincts, panthers are mainly ambush predators, preying on large deer and, in South America, the capybara (a large rodent). Despite being the pre-eminent feline in Canada and North America, the panther is considered not to be an apex predator as it must interact and compete with the brown bear and packs of wolves. Heavily featured in the mythology of indigenous peoples of both American continents, it is sometimes seen as a harbinger of death.

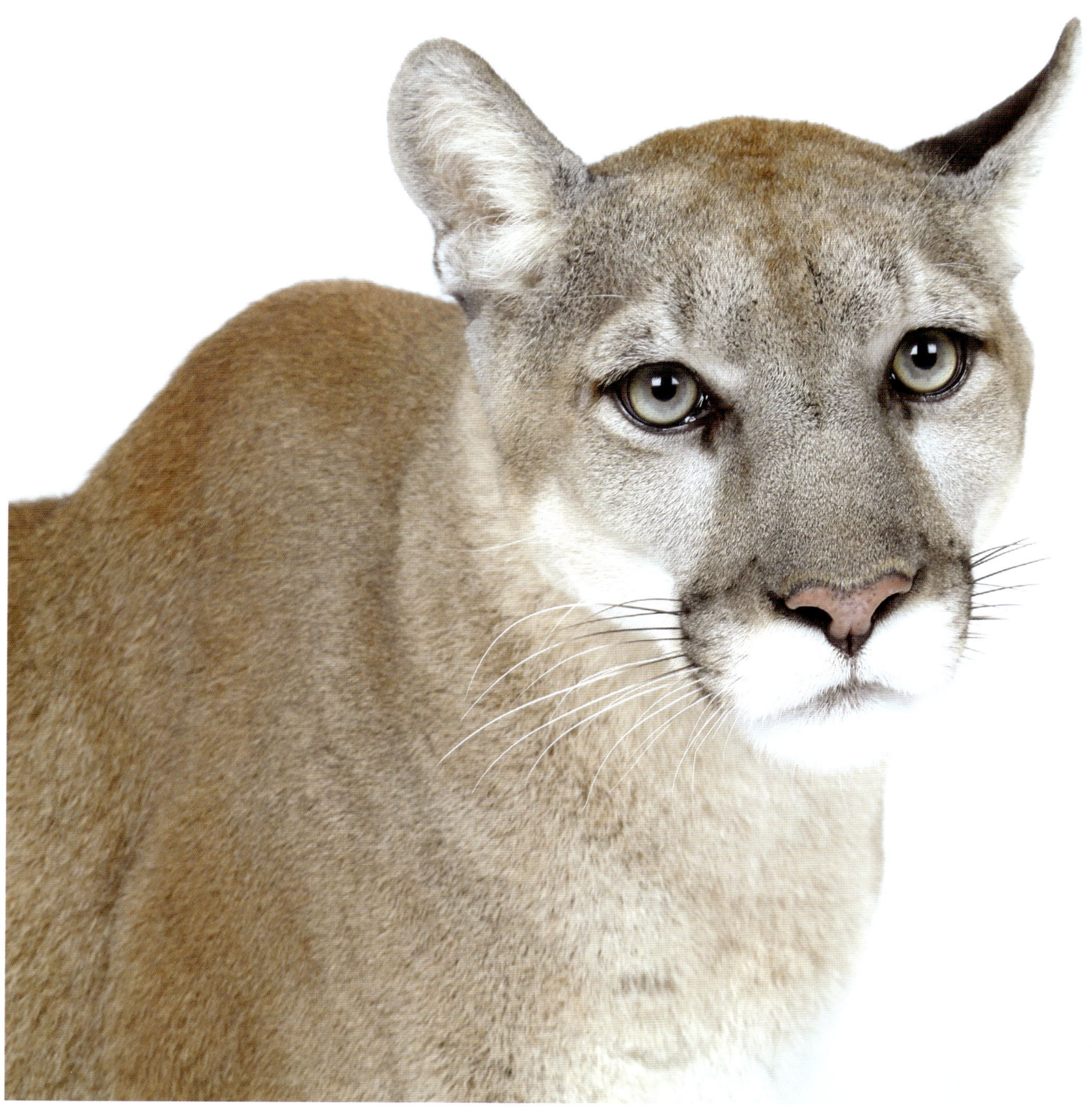

Panthers have a lifespan of around 8 to 13 years in the wild and up to 20 years in captivity.

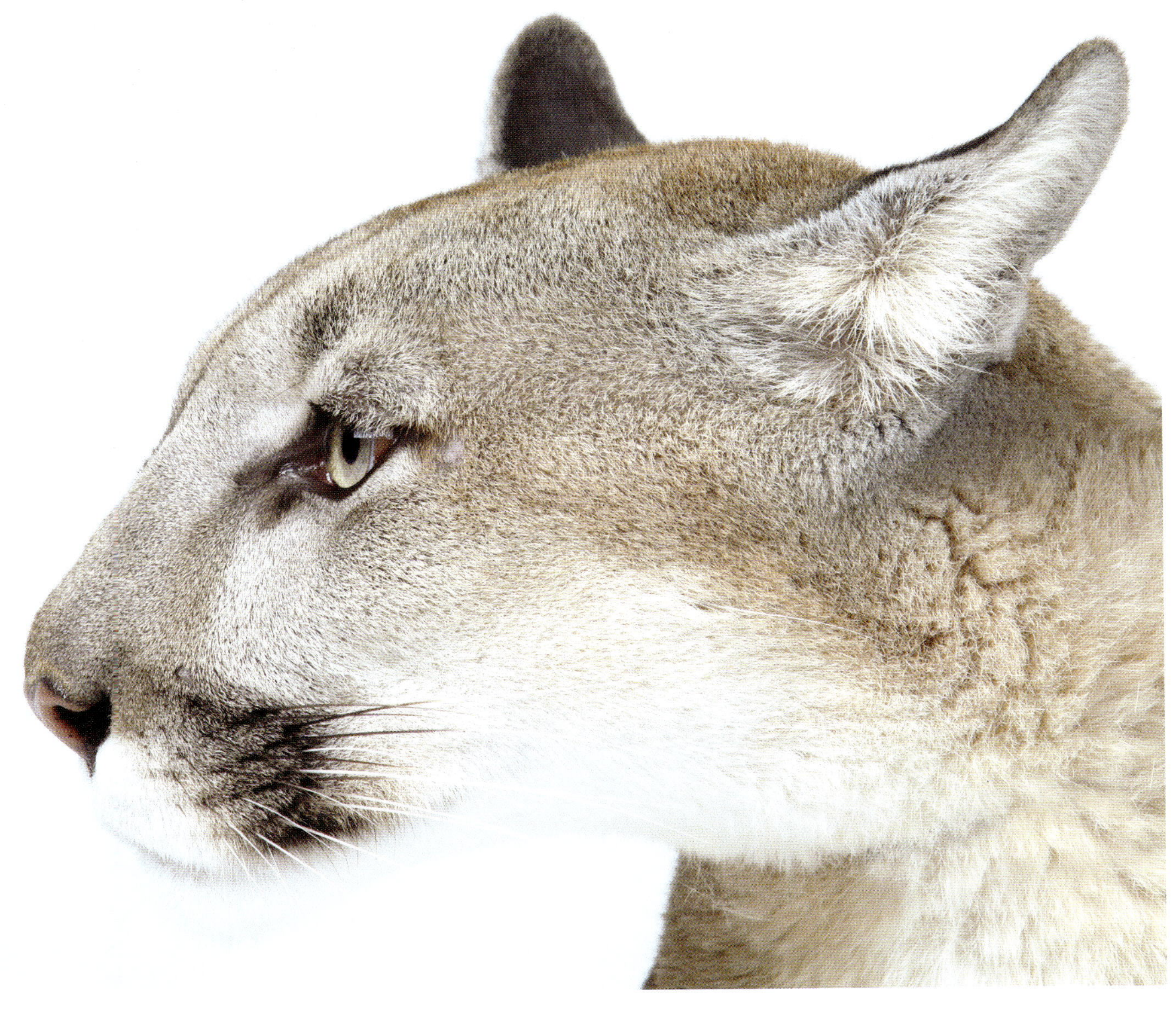

Unlike other big cats, panthers cannot roar. They hiss, growl and sometimes even scream.

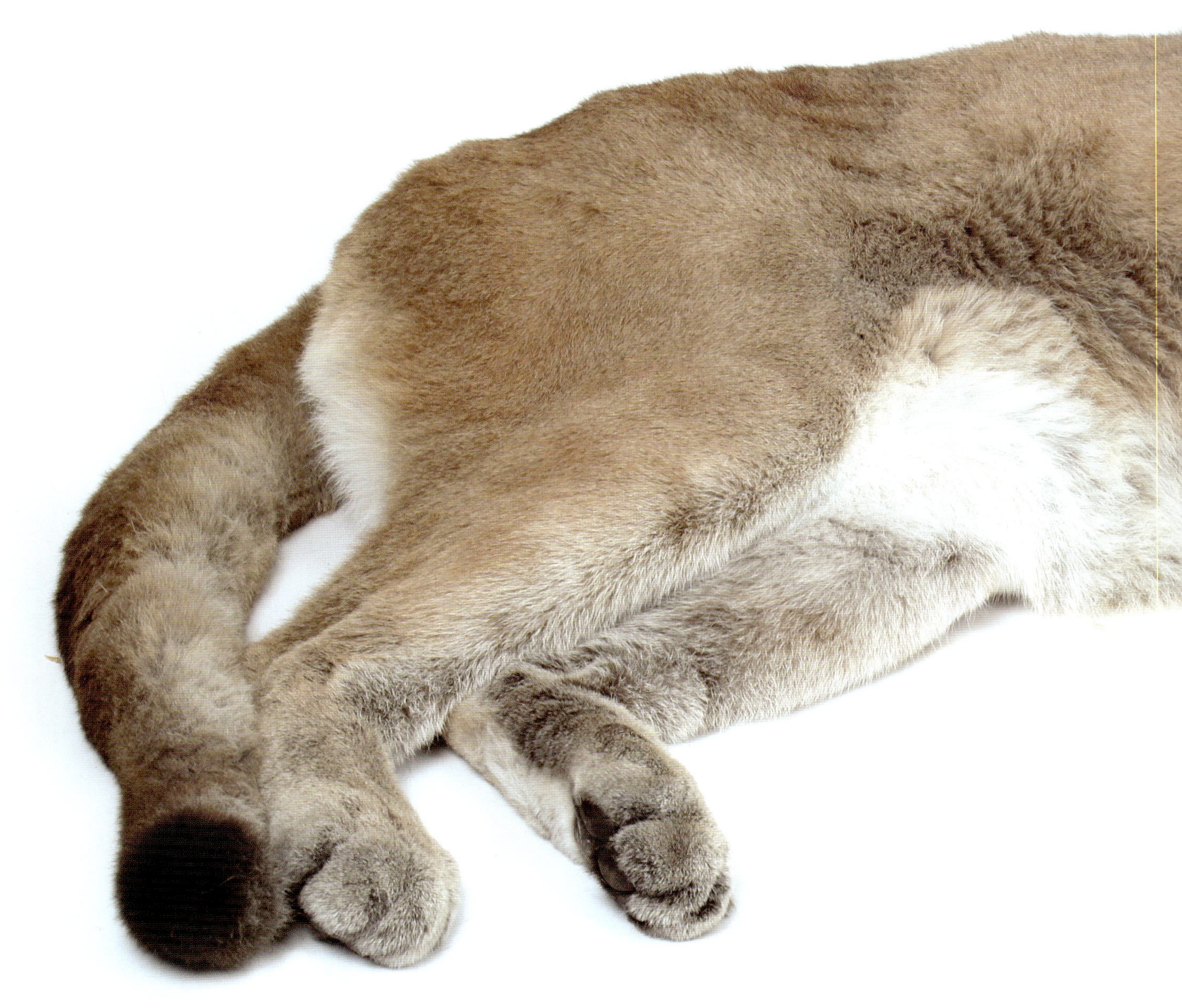

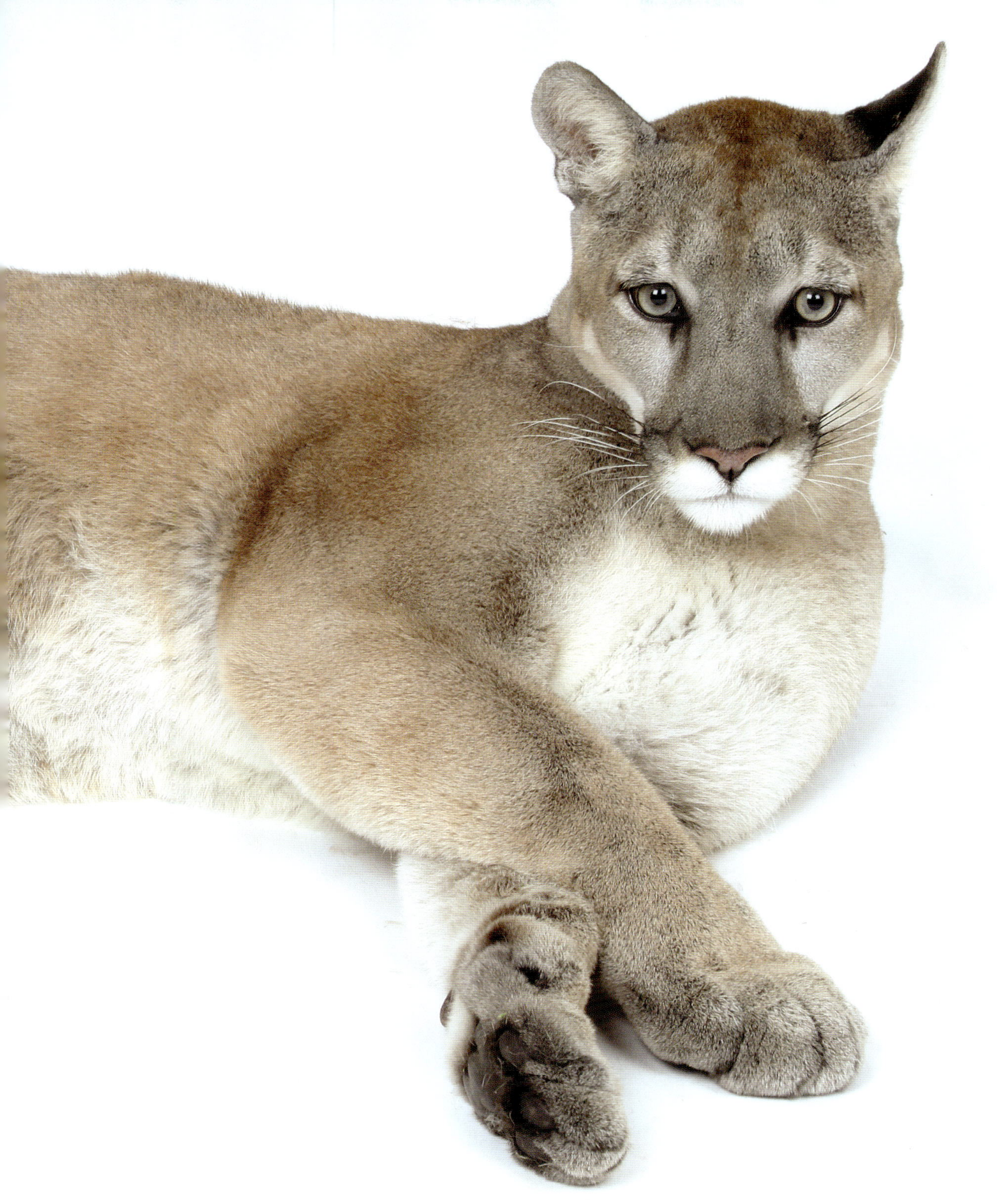

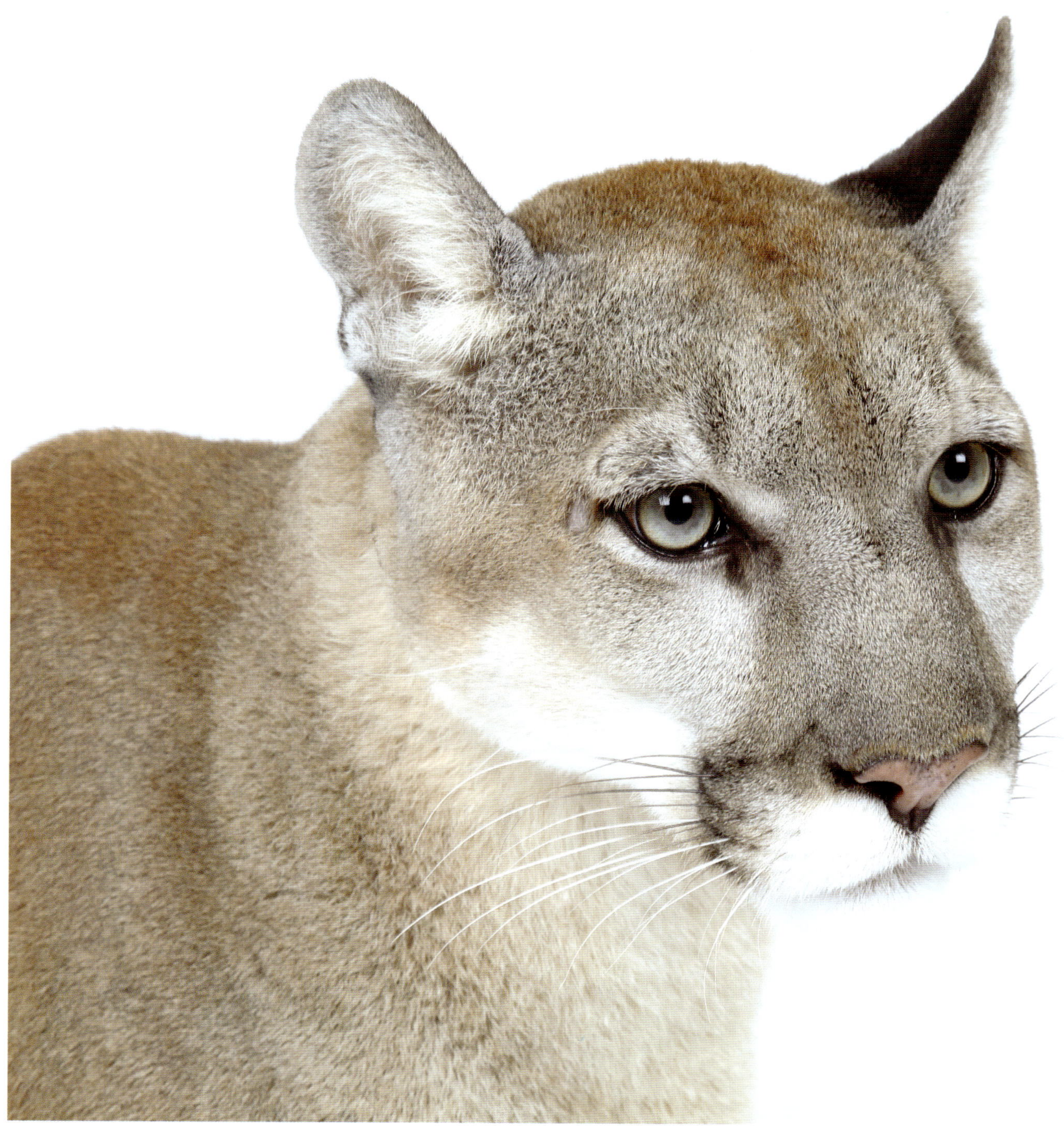

As human populations encroach upon the natural habitat of the panther, attacks on livestock are more common.

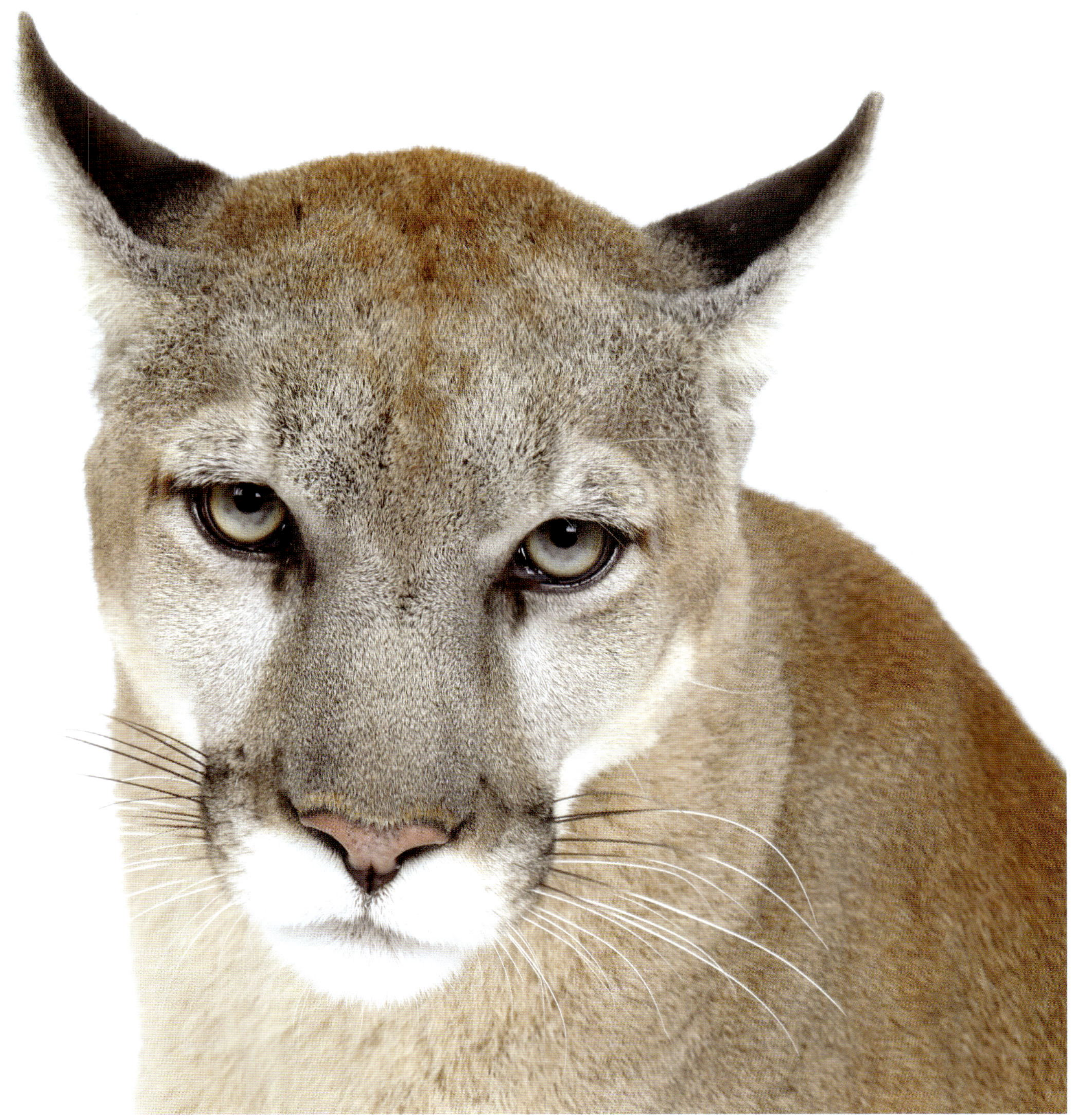

Black panther' is a colloquial name for other types of cat, such as the leopard, that have black colouring (melanism).

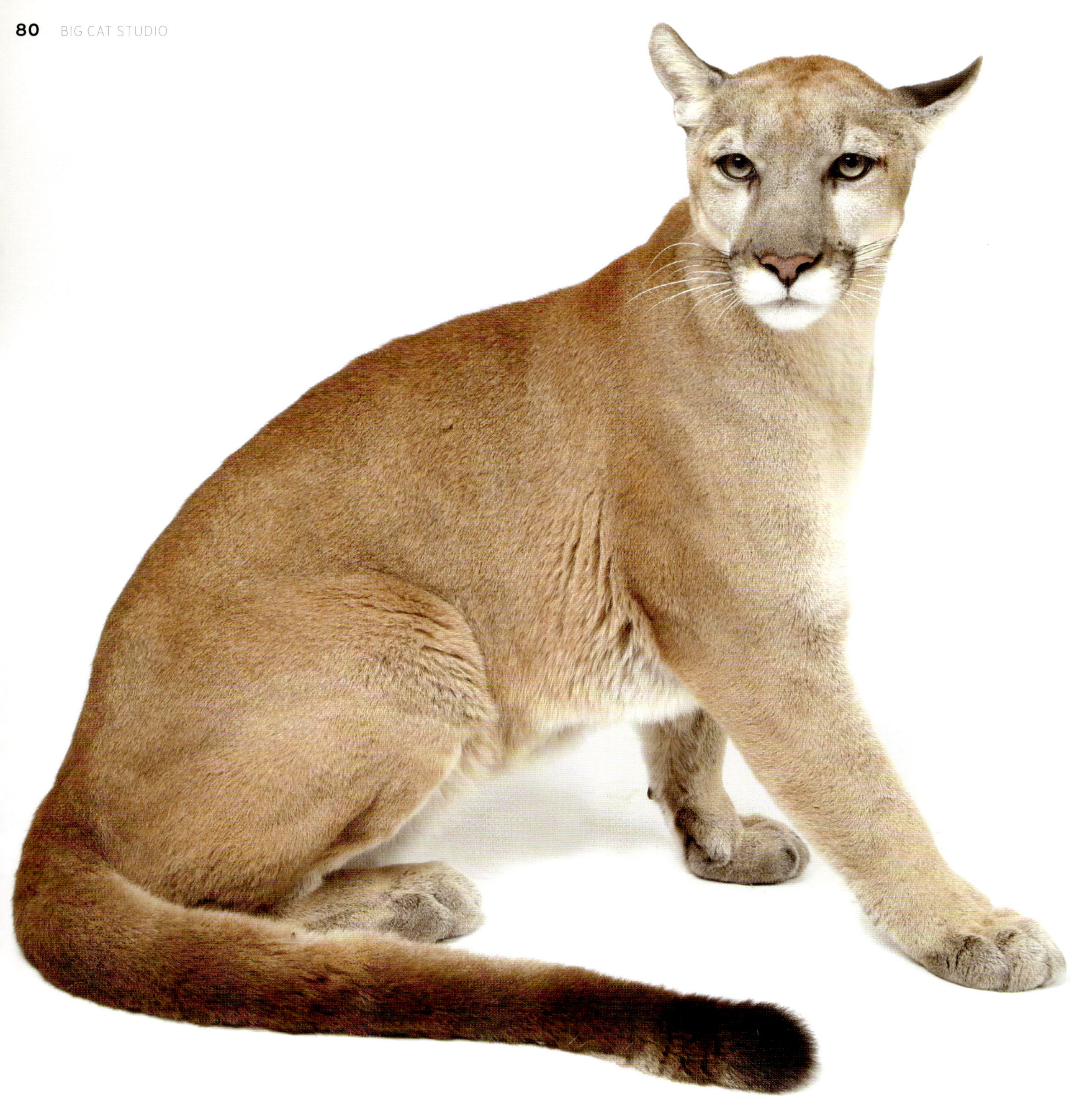

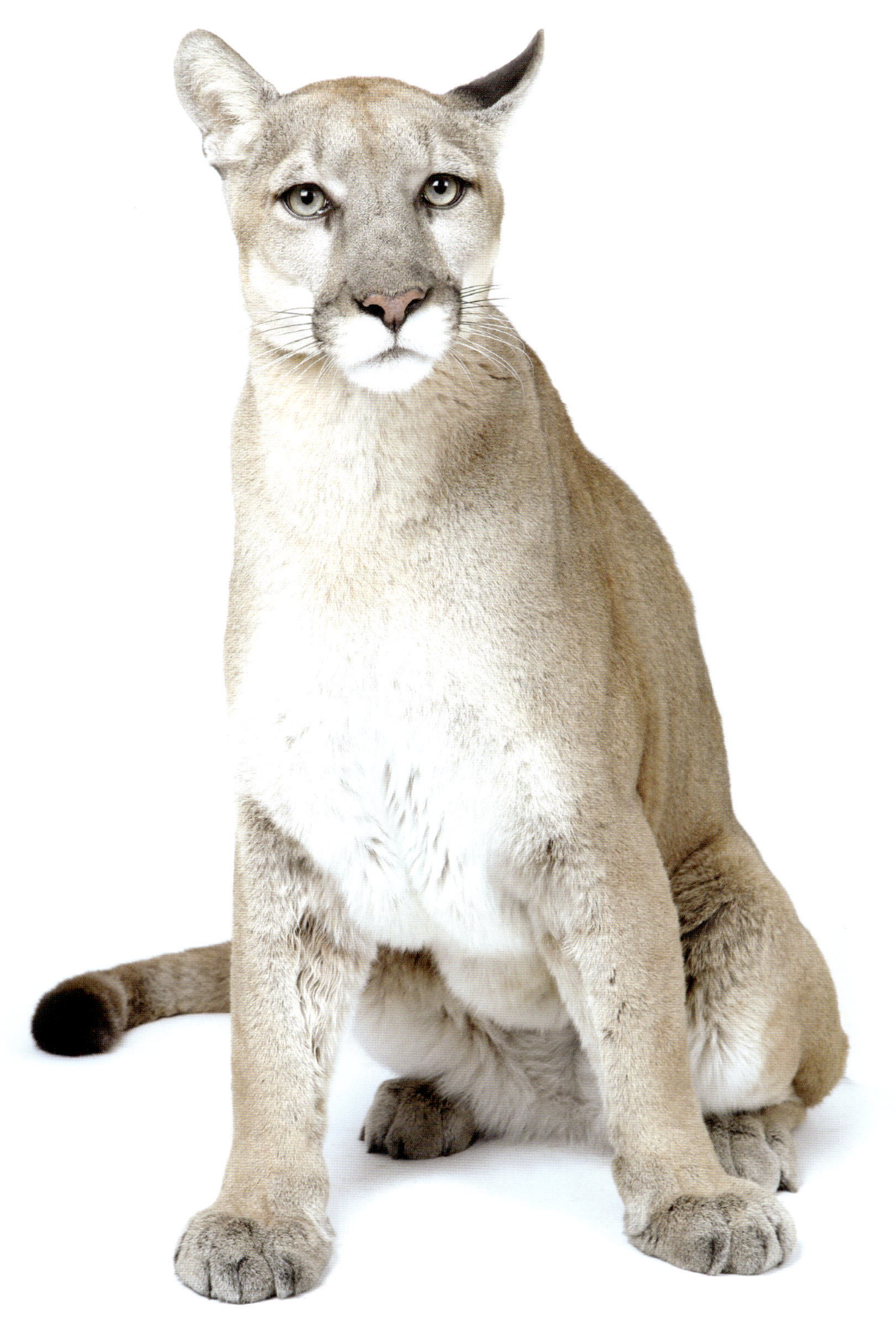

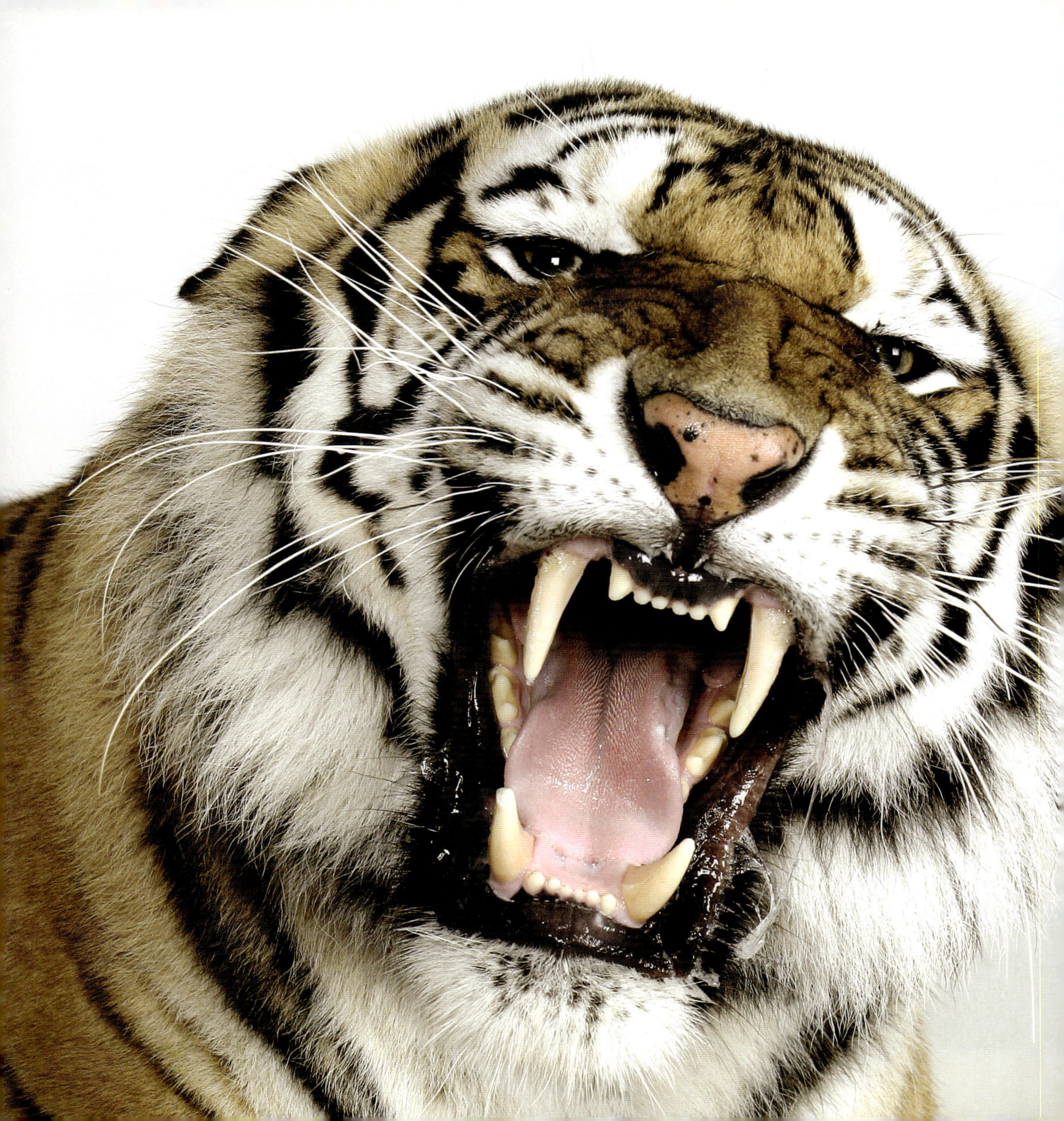

TIGER

Found across much of eastern and southern Asia, there are currently six active sub-species of tiger, of which the Royal Bengal is the most numerous and the Siberian the largest. Classed as endangered, it is estimated that less than 10,000 tigers are currently living in the wild; this century alone, two distinct sub-species of tiger, the Balinese and the Javan have become extinct. The largest of all big cats, the tiger can reach up to 13ft (4m) from head to tail and weigh up to 660lb (300kg). Their natural habitat can clash with some of man's most densely populated regions and has led to conflict between humans and tigers. The fabled man-eating tigers that have found notoriety in India and Bangladesh are generally older tigers who have lost the ability to chase and catch more fleet-footed prey such as wild boar. Vulnerable to poachers keen to sell body parts as medicines in Asia, tigers are actively protected by the state governments of the countries in which they live.

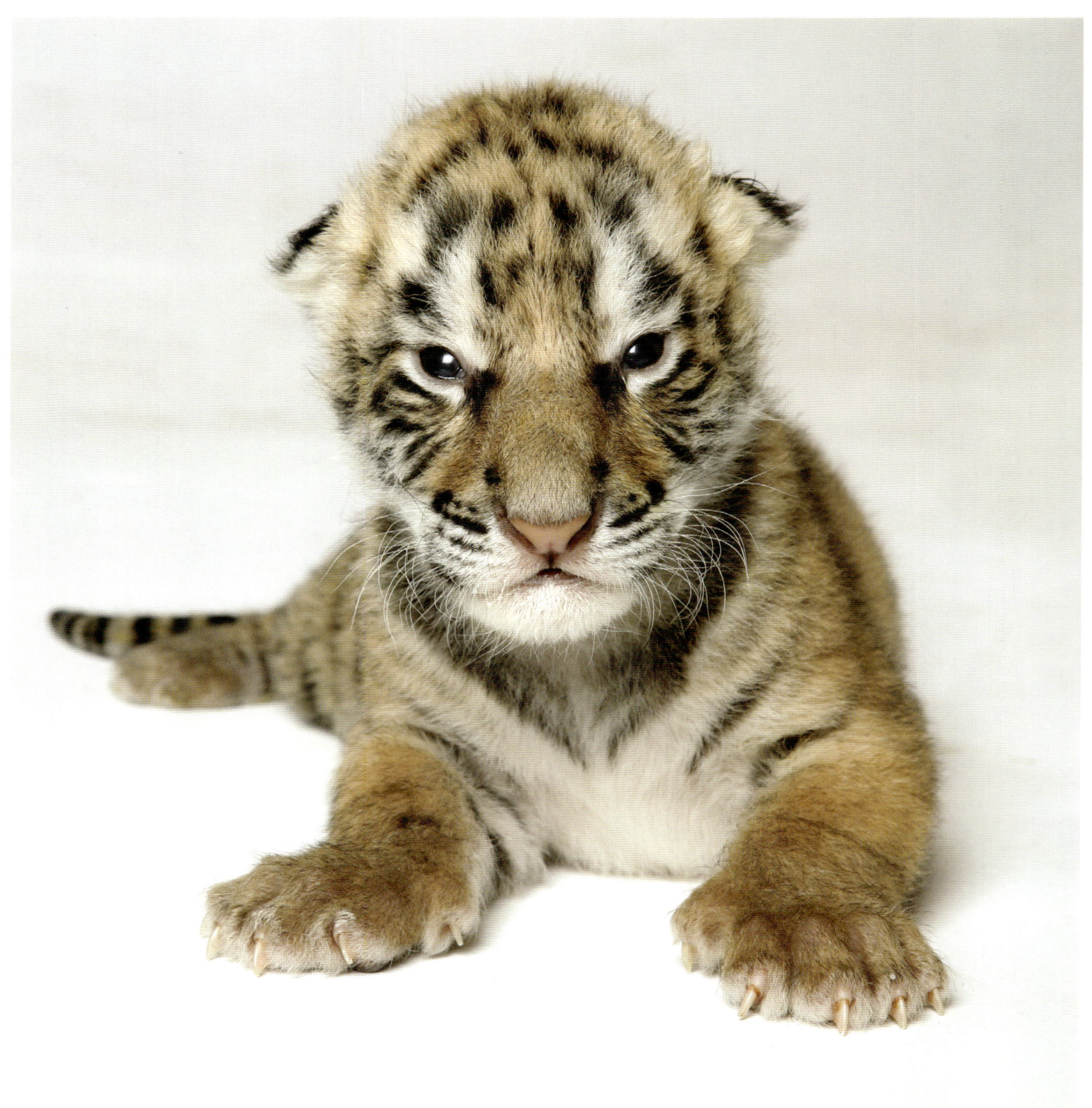

Tiger cubs are born blind and will not leave the den to explore until they are eight weeks old.

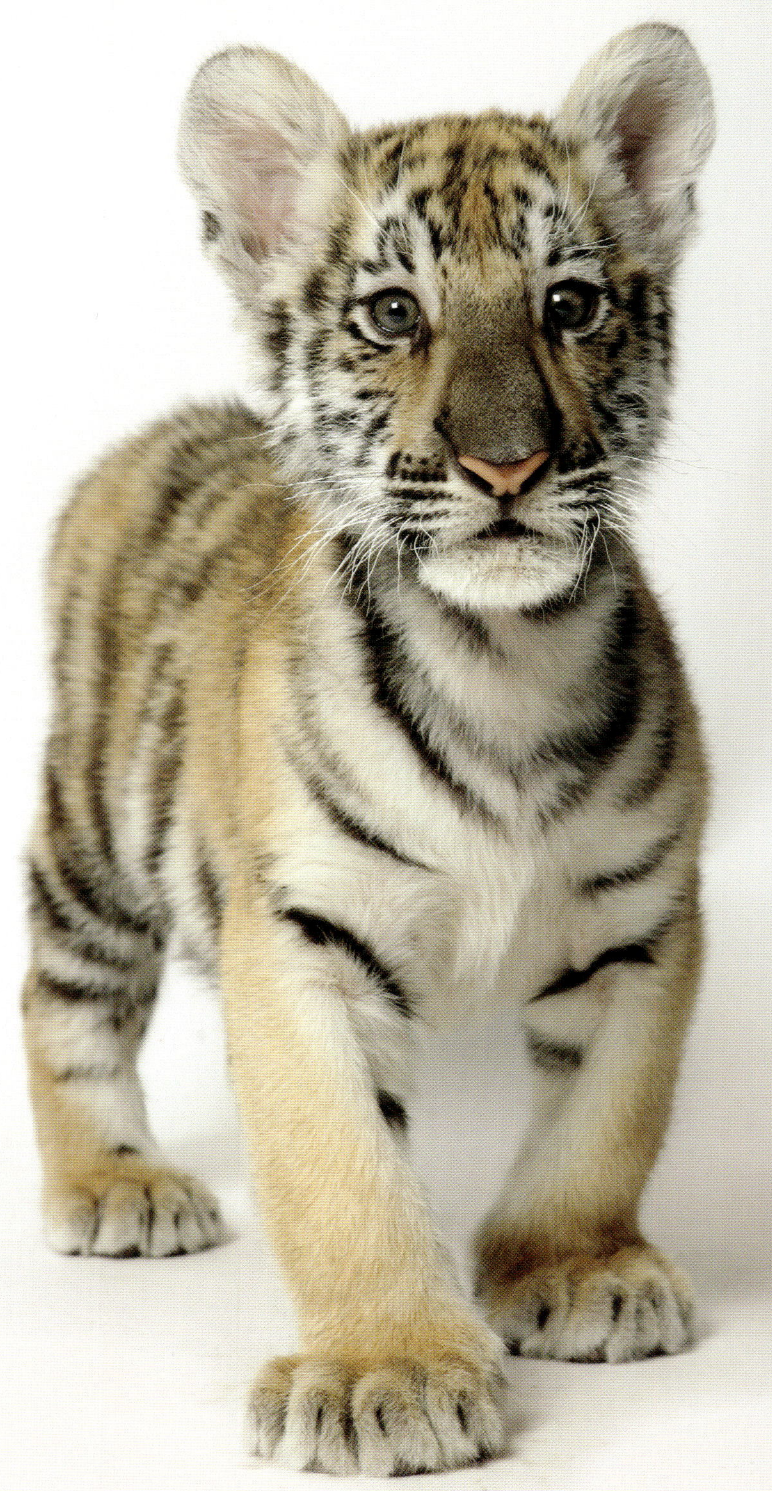

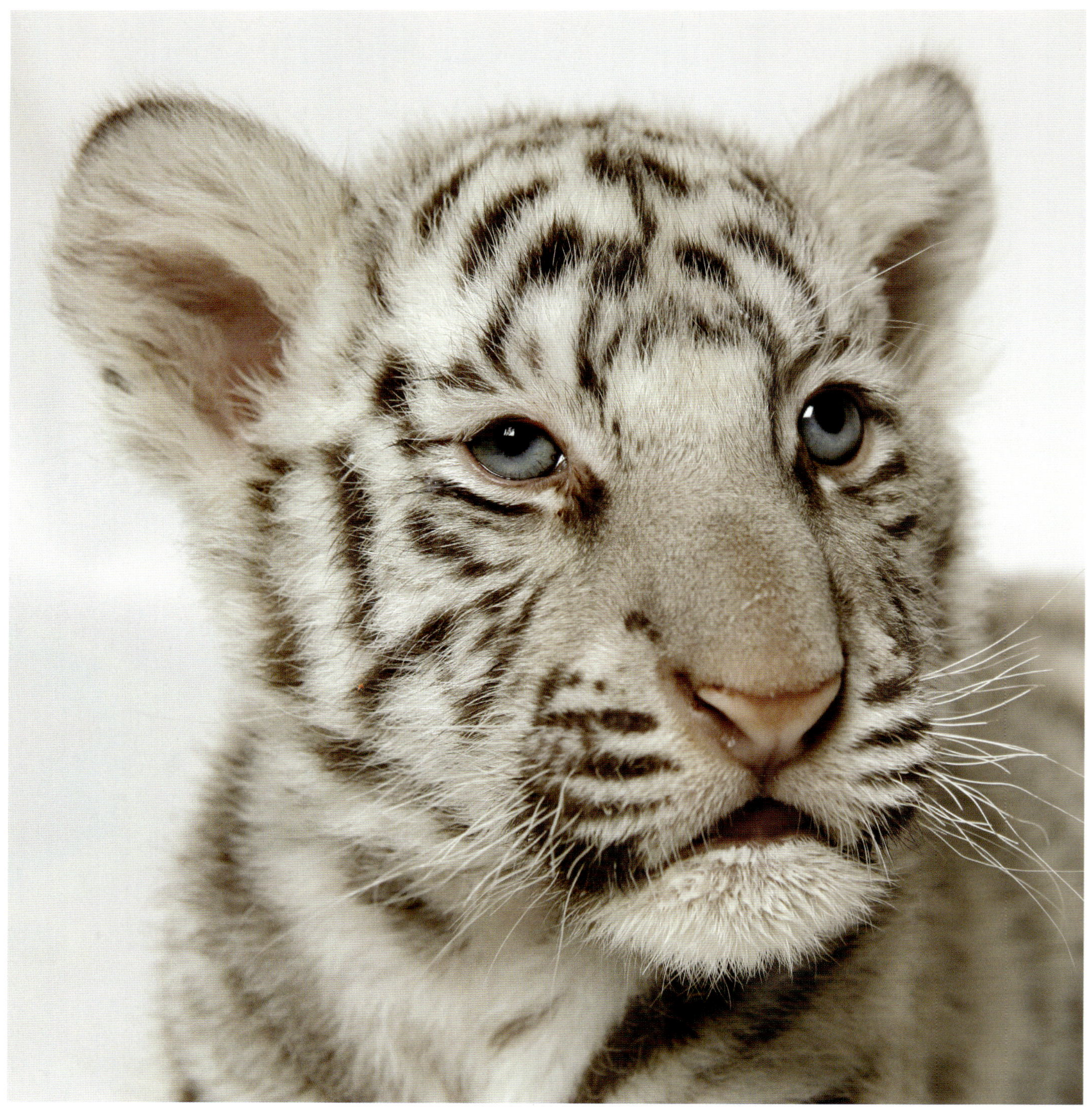

Cubs are always raised by the female tiger as male tigers are often regarded as predators.

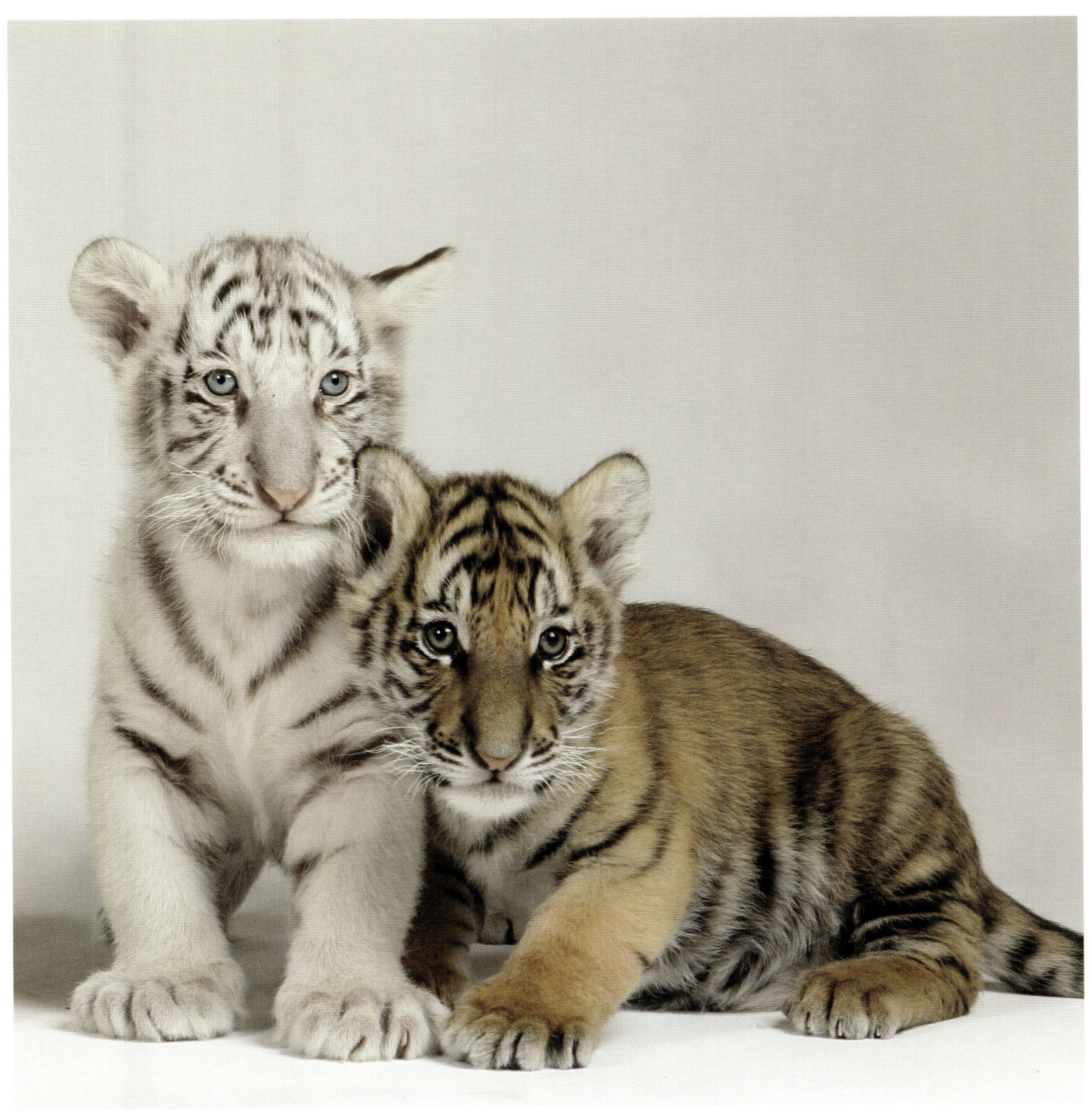

Tiger cubs are highly prized by poachers for their valuable coats and other body parts.

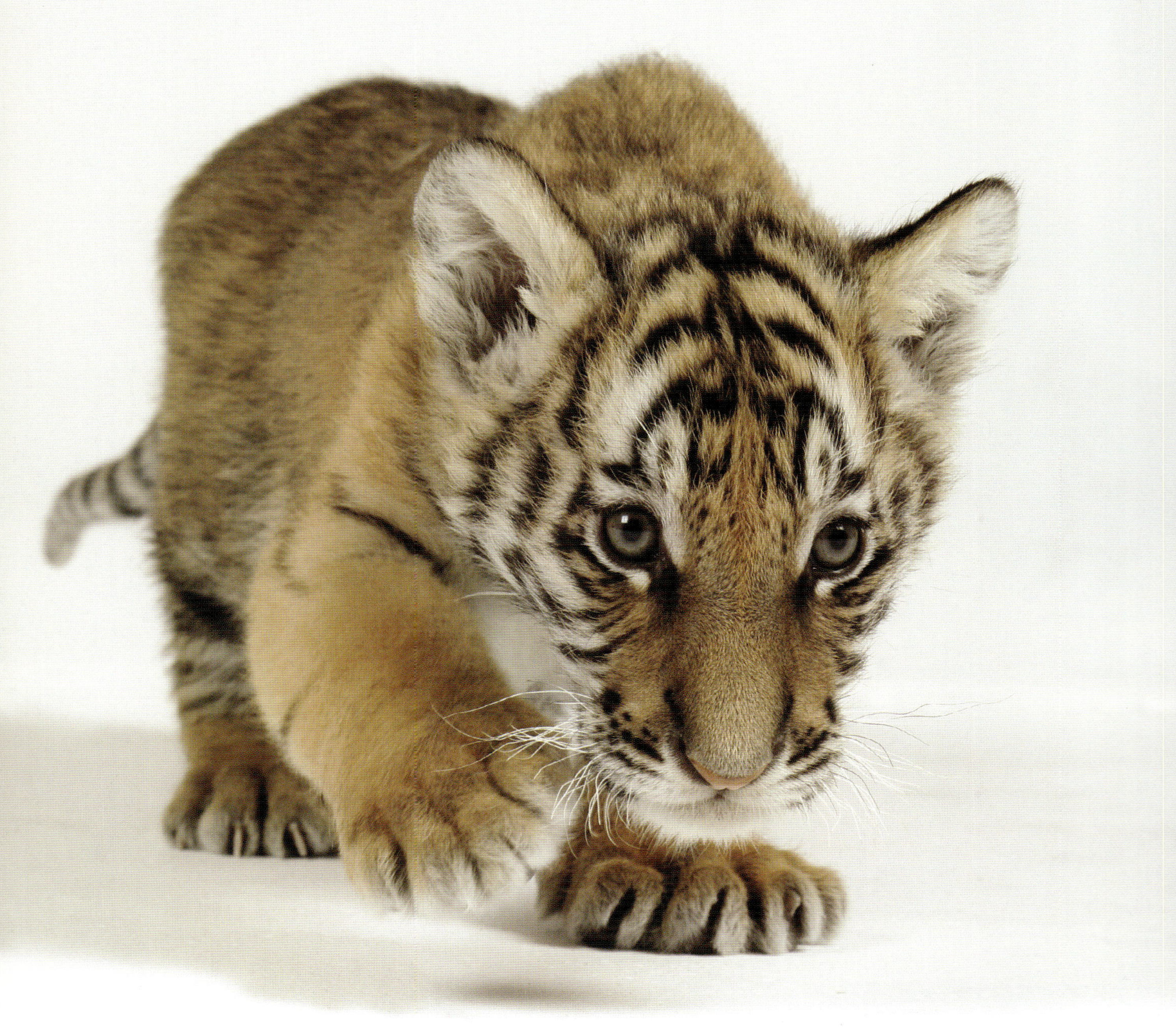

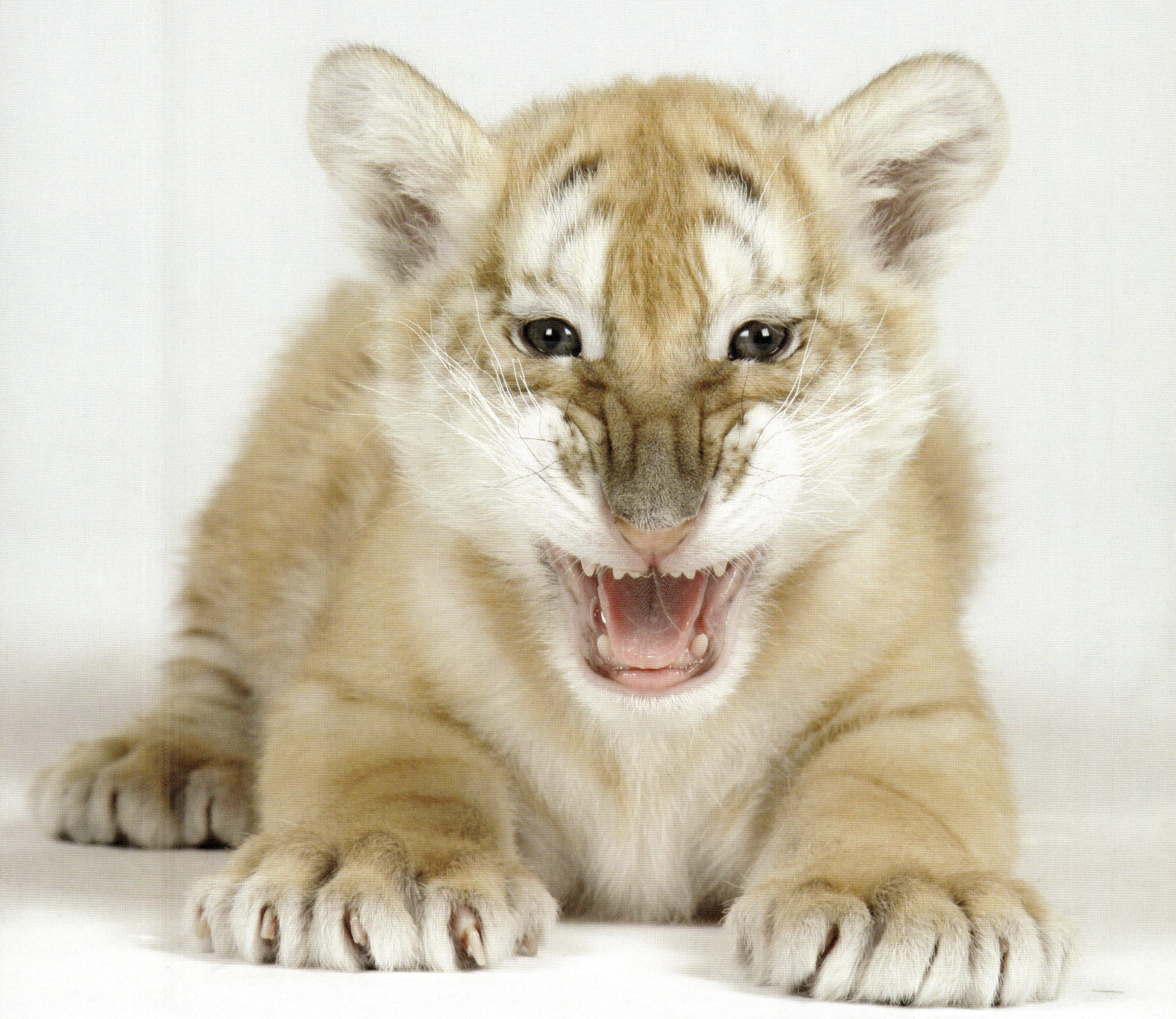

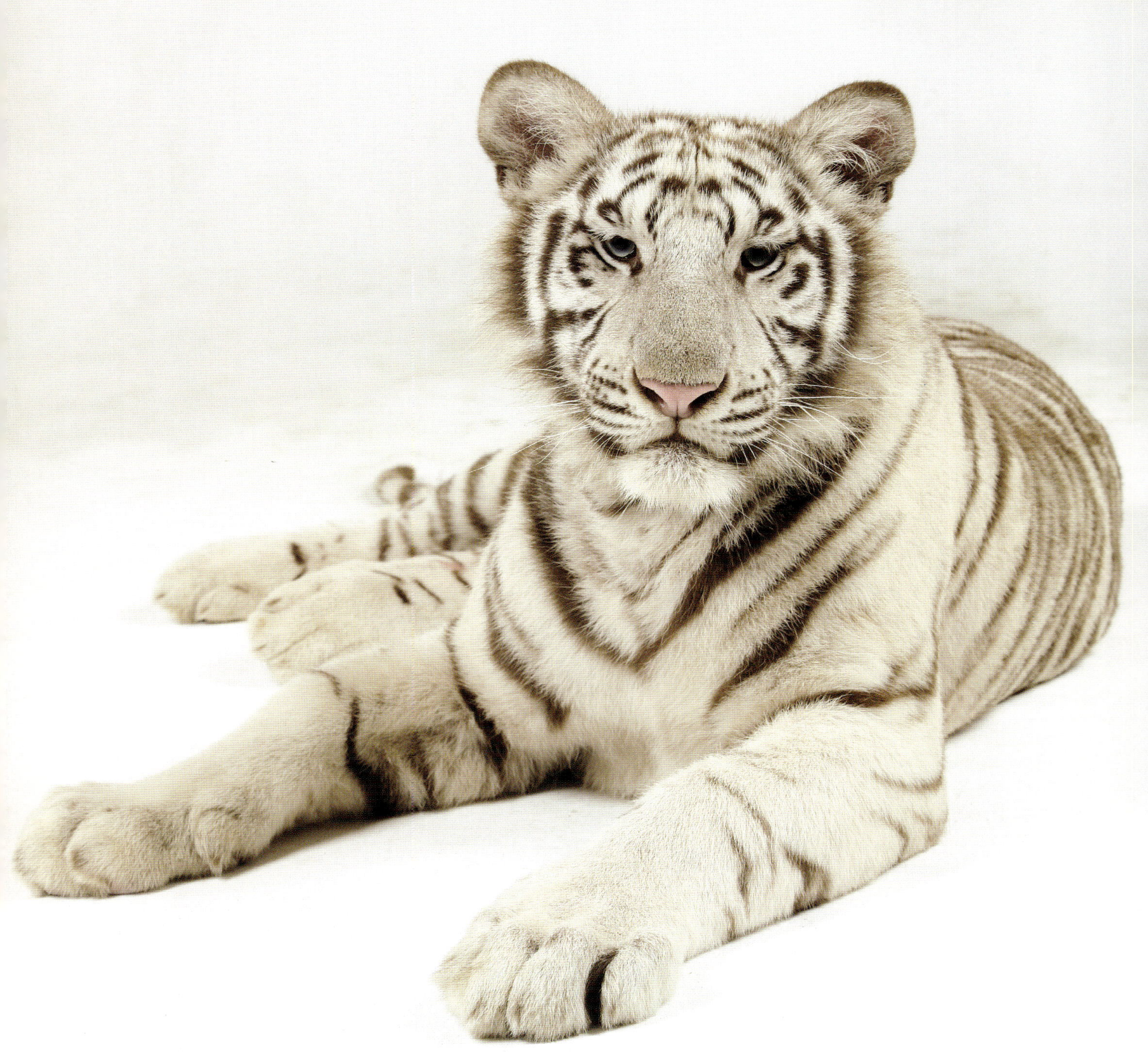

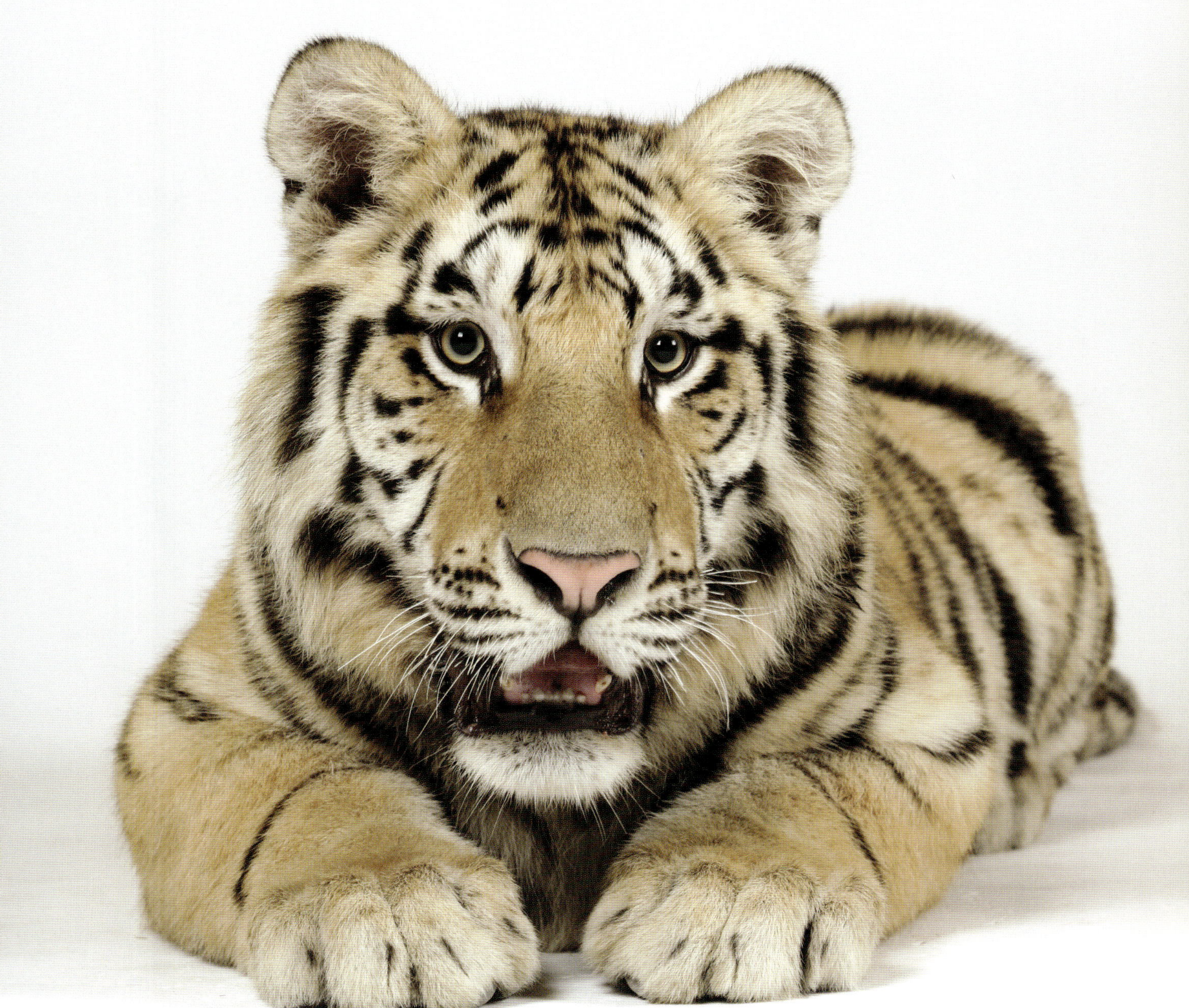

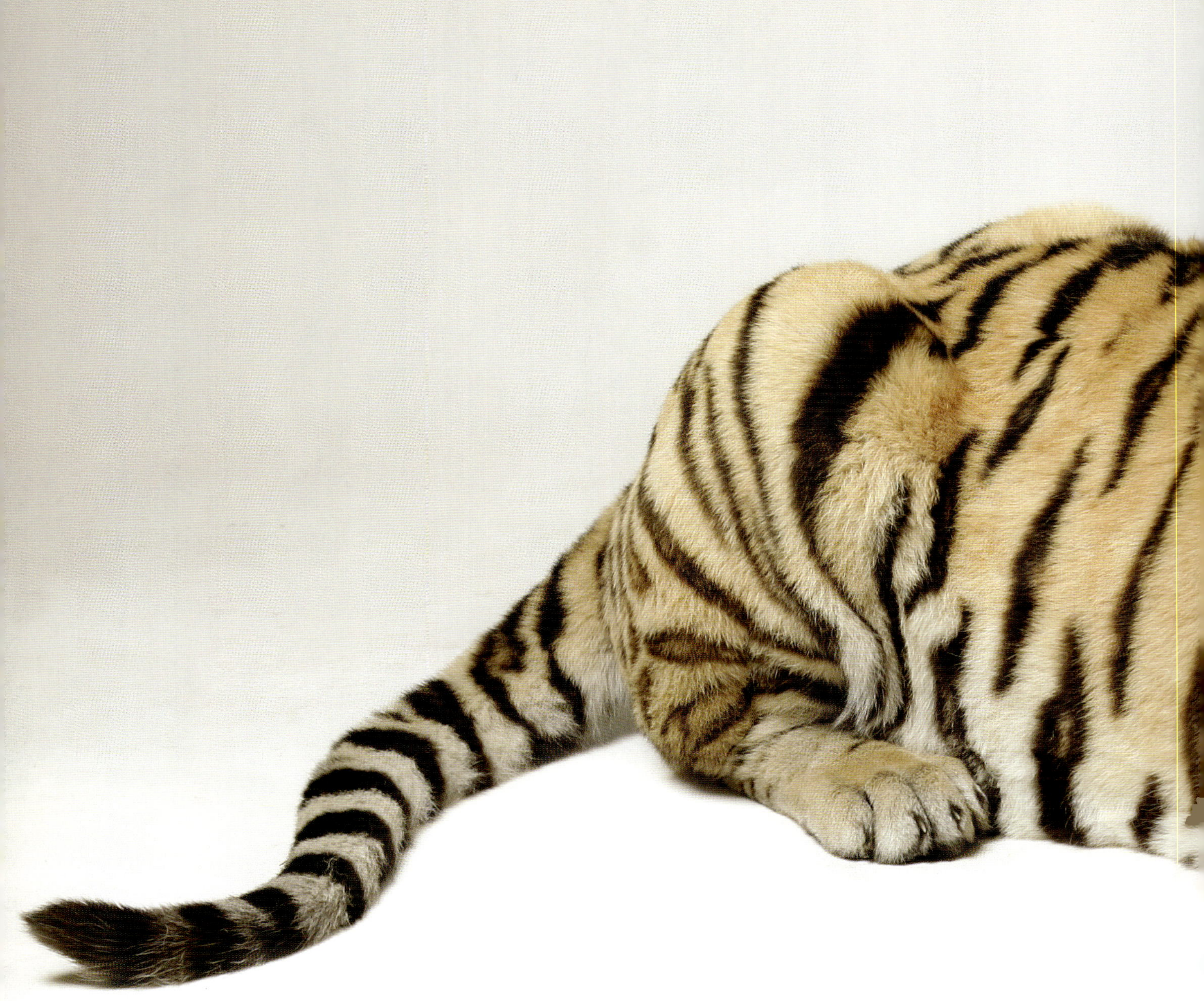

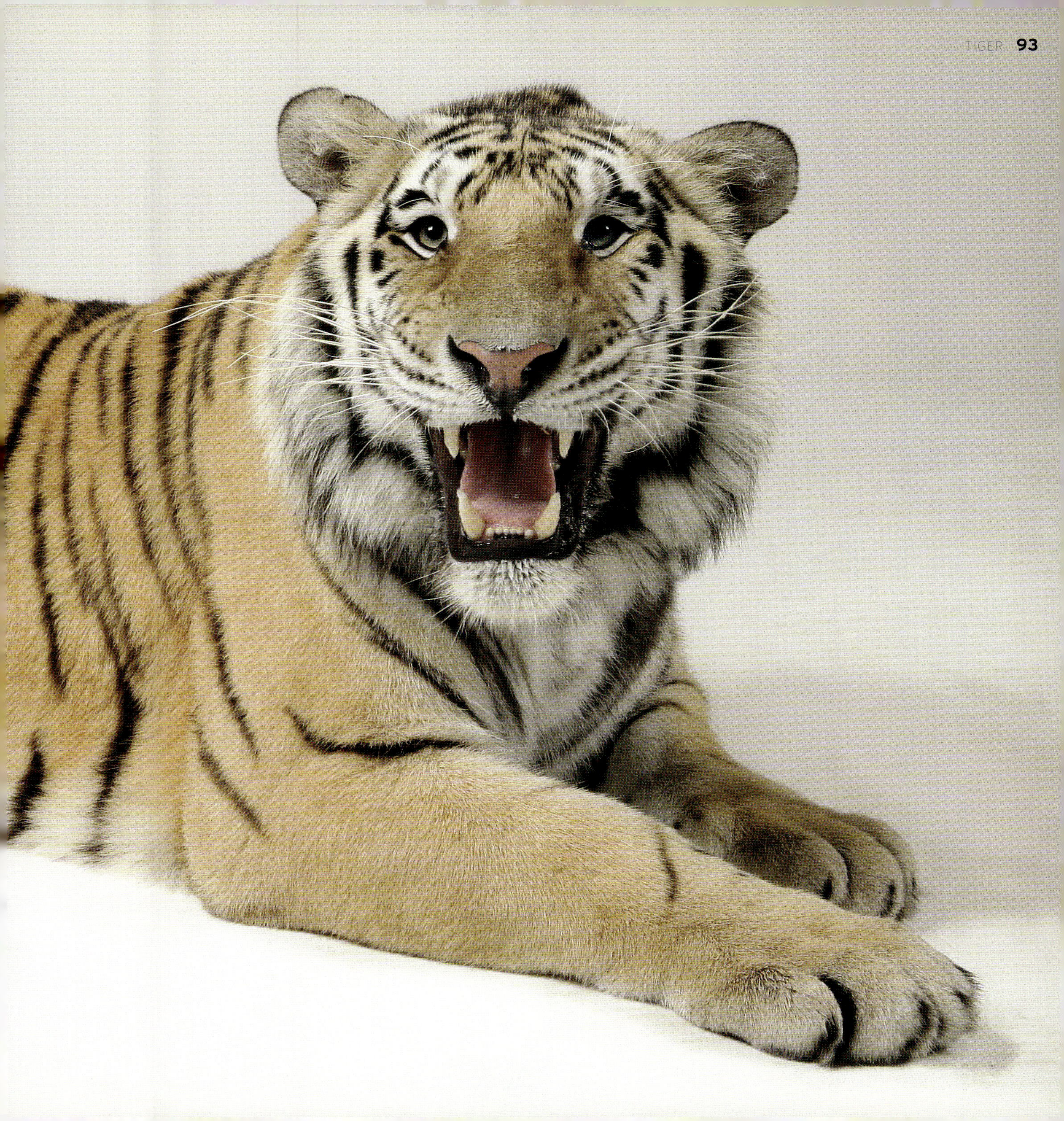

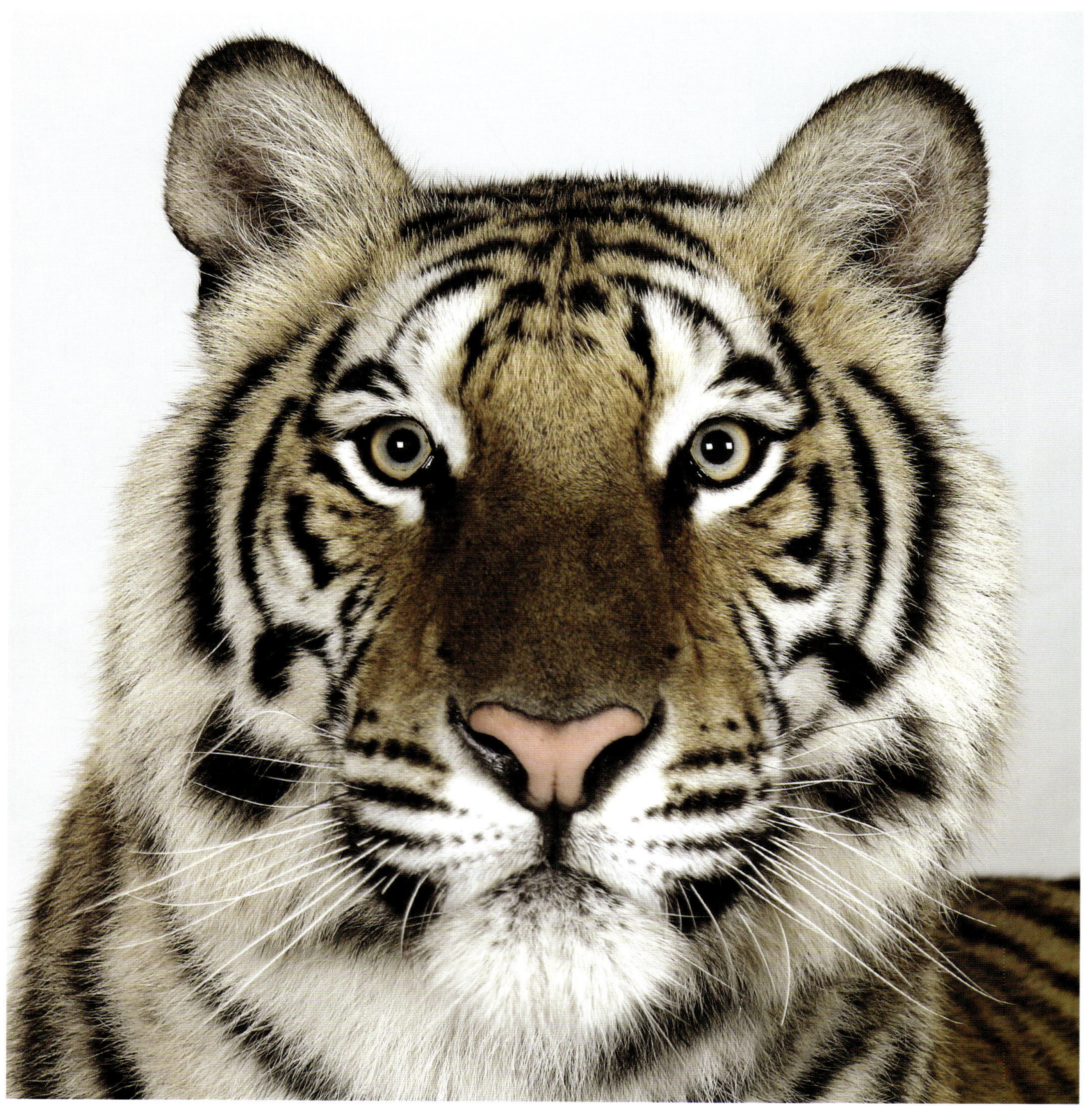

With their dark stripes and powerful build, tigers have entered into the traditional stories and culture of many Asian nations.

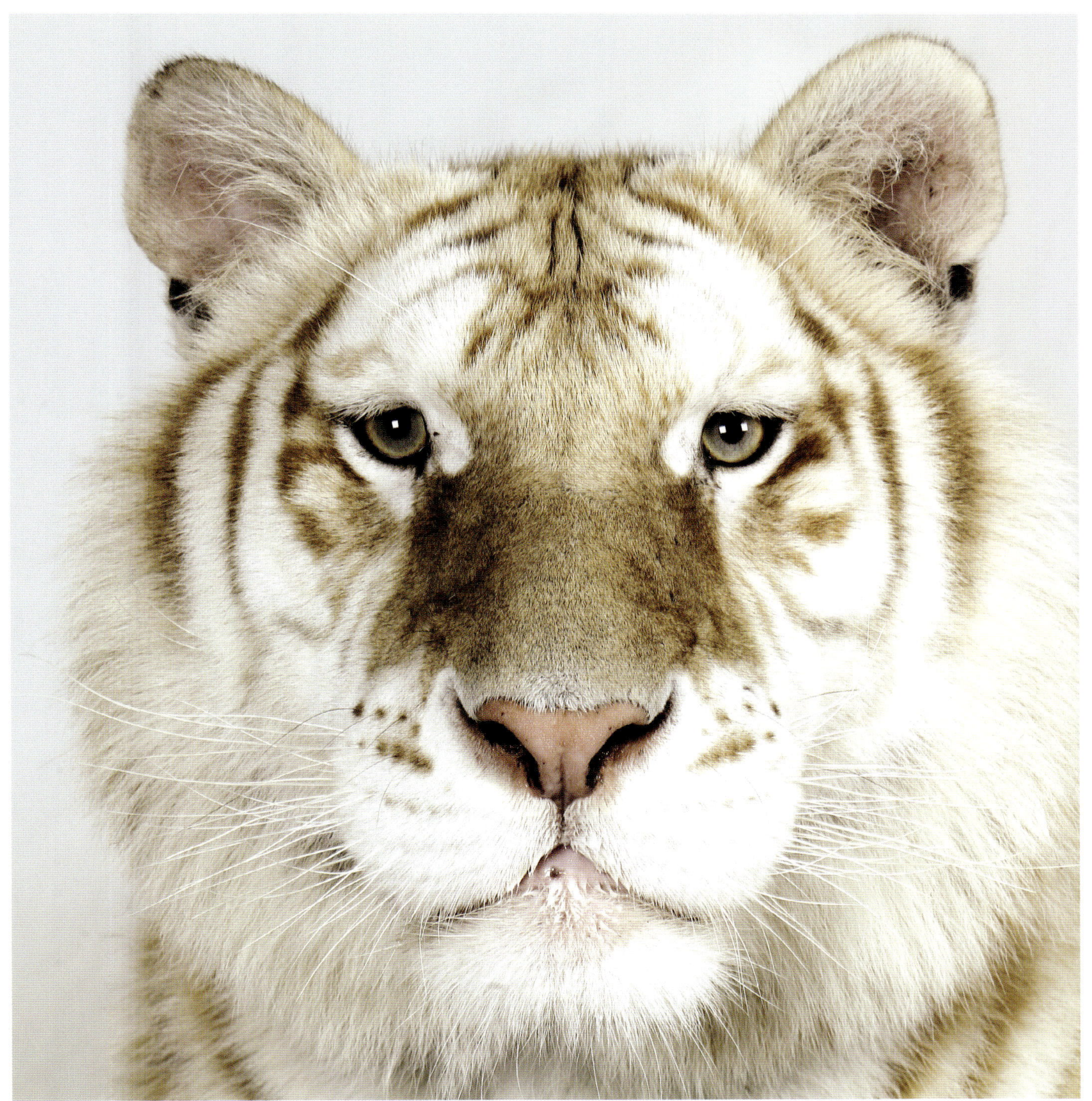

In Asian folklore the whiskers of a tiger are believed to bestow courage and protection on the wearer.

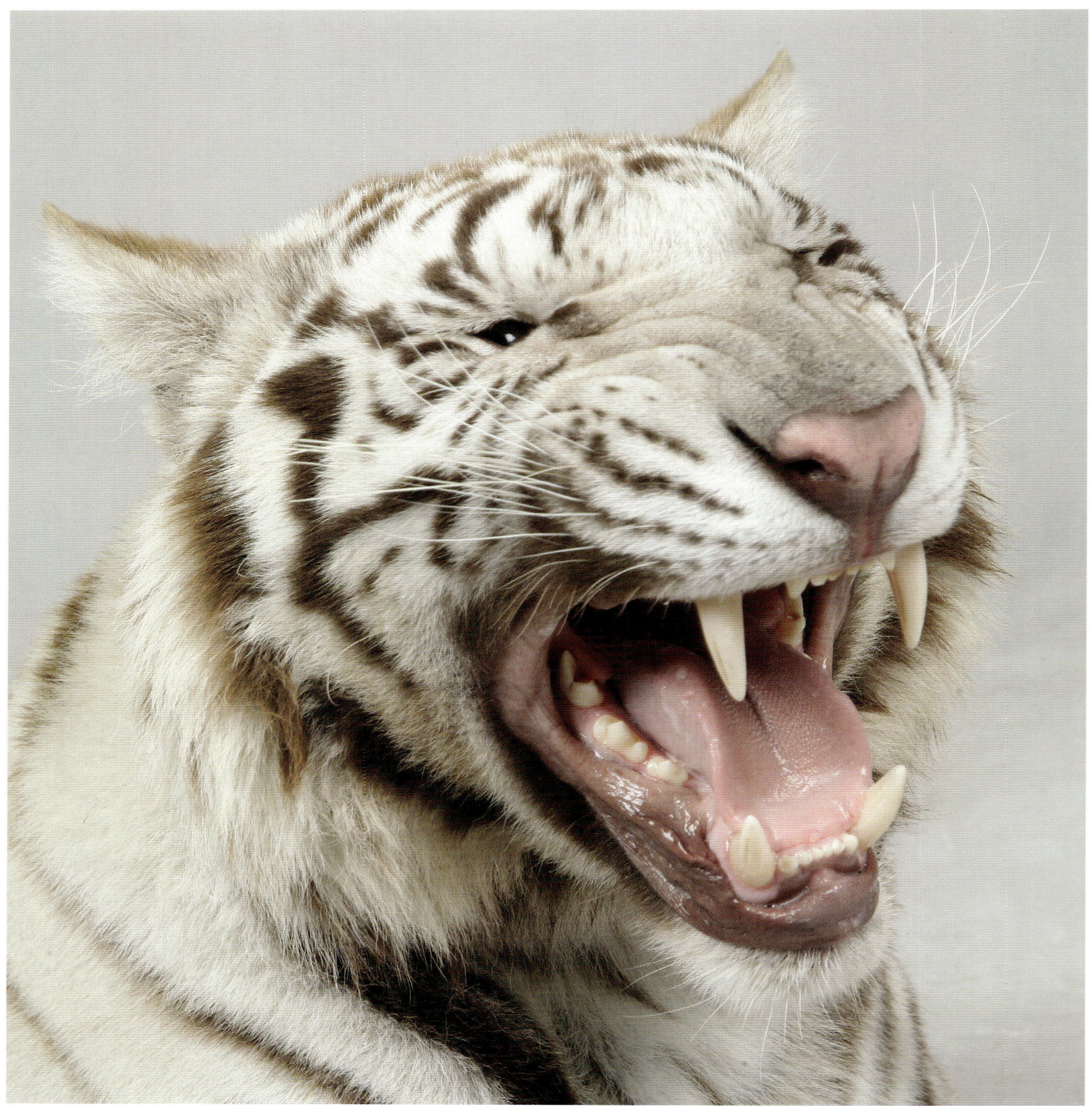

In the wild, tigers are solitary hunters relying on their eyesight and sense of smell to track down their prey.

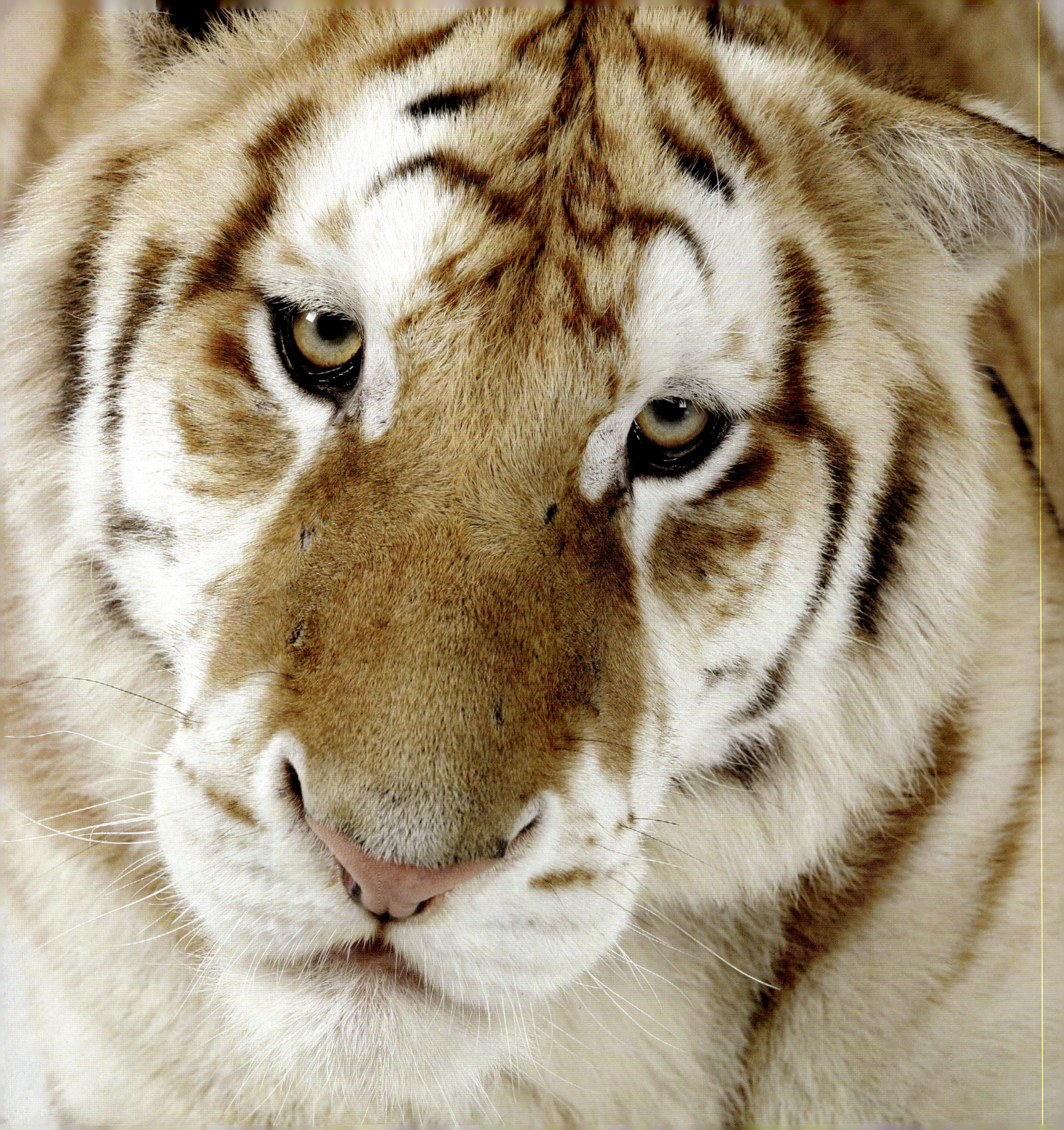

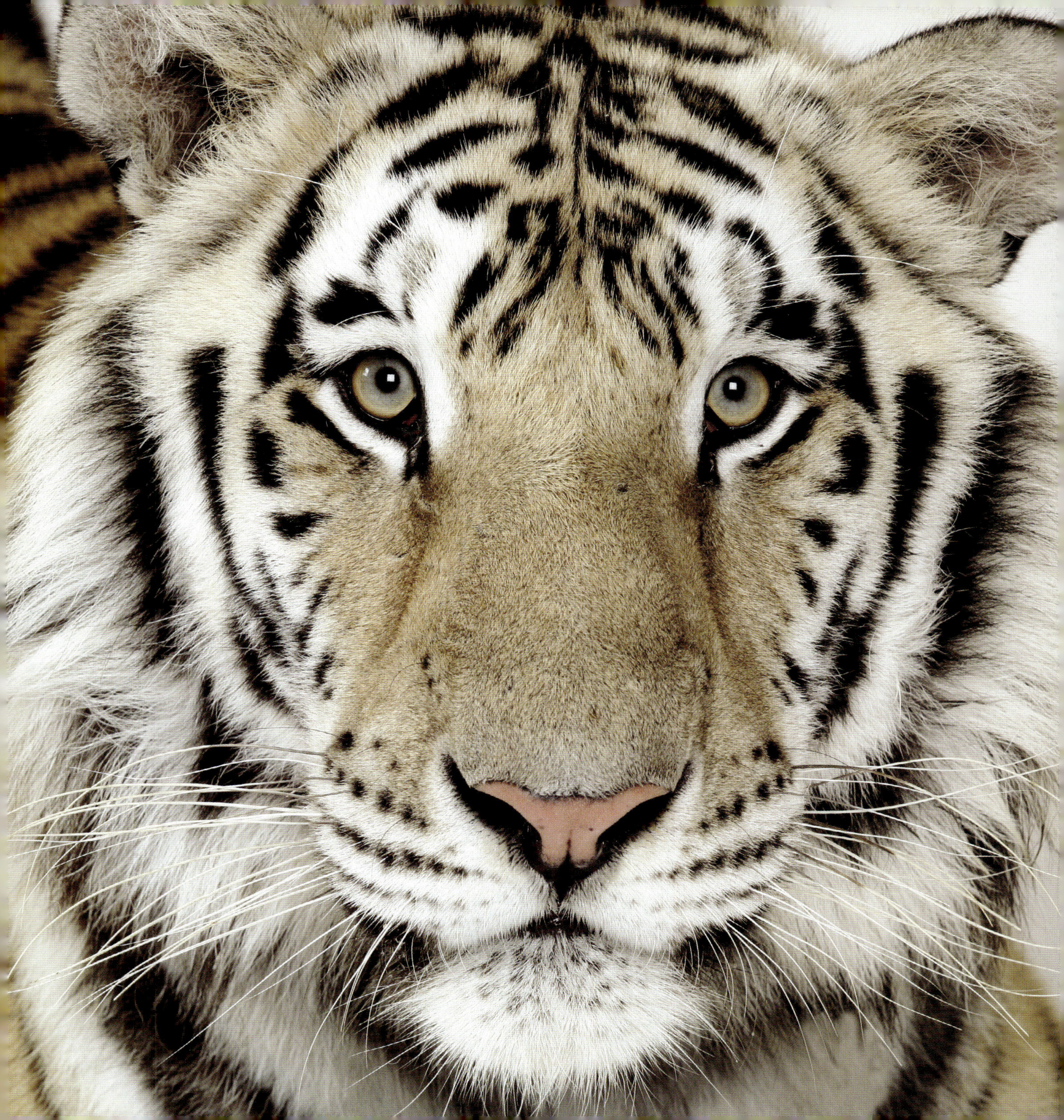

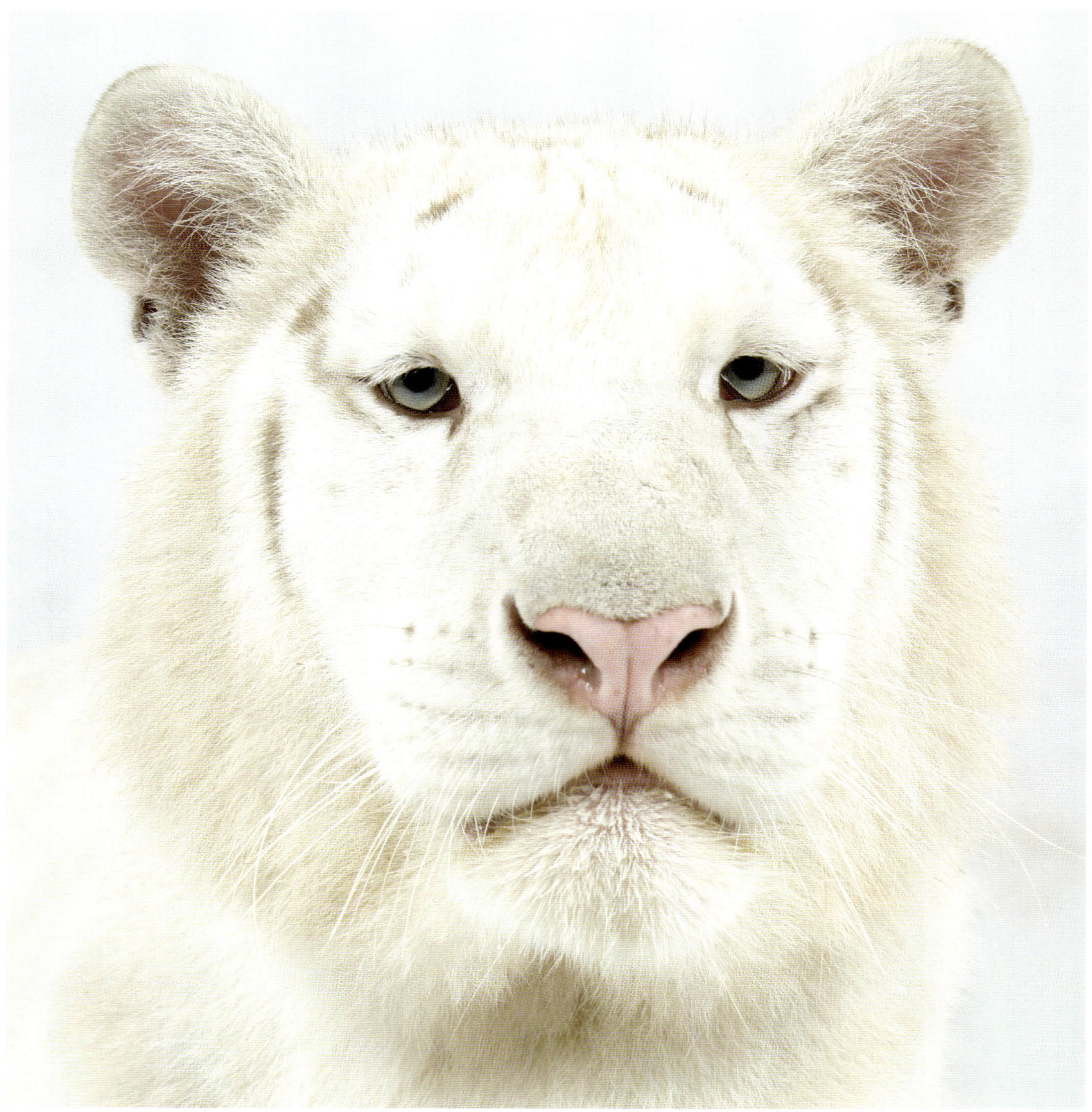

White tigers are not a separate sub-species, they occur when both parents carry the unusual gene for whiteness.

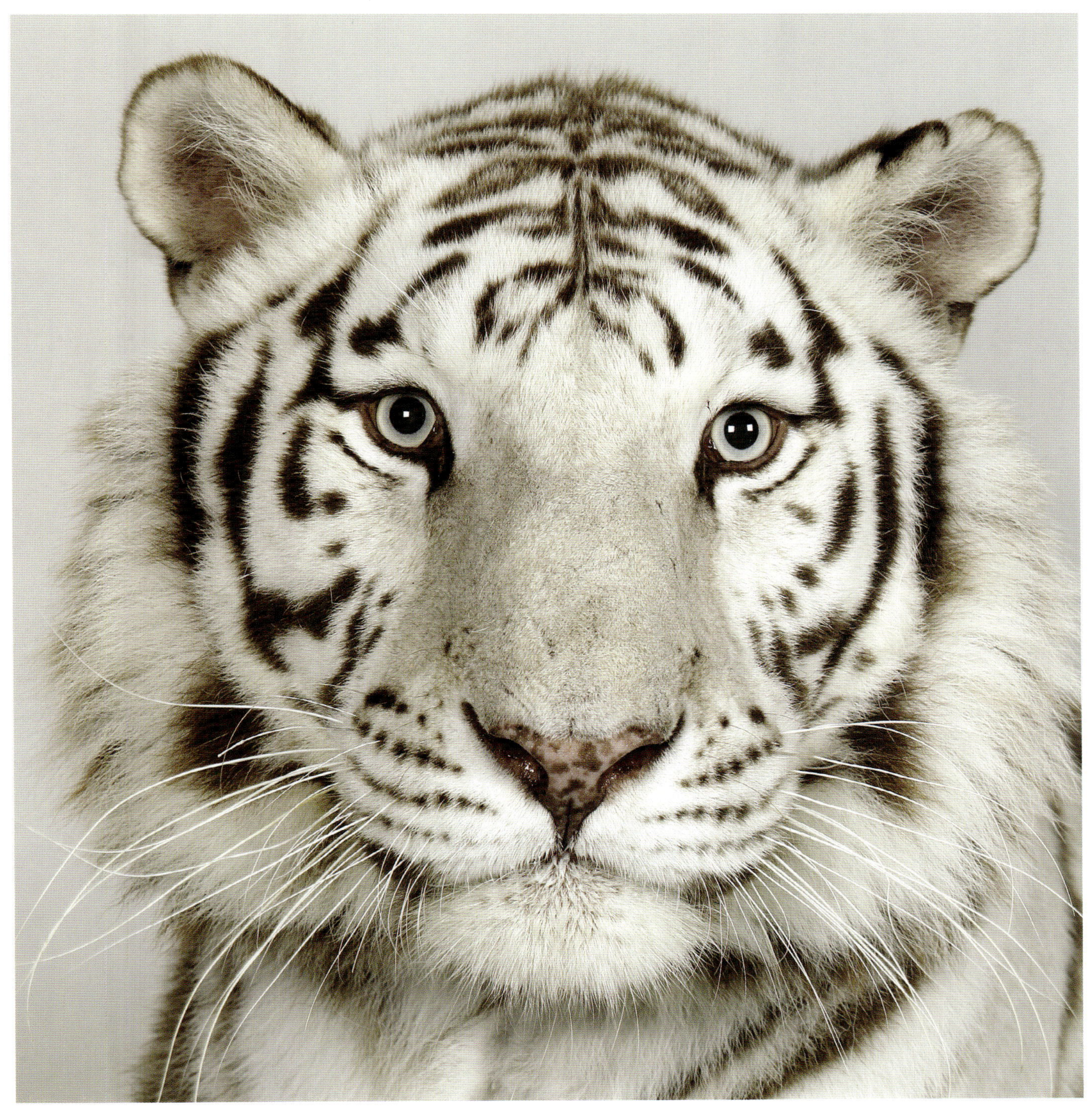

Like domestic cats, tigers spend a large part of the day sleeping and resting (up to 20 hours a day).

CAT PROFILES

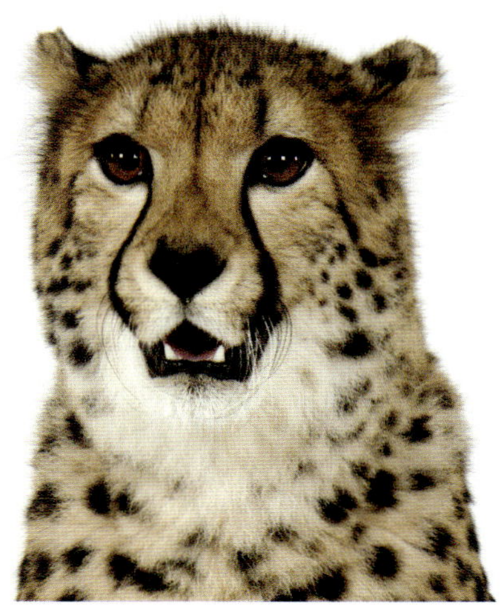

CLEOPATRA

Cheetah
Acinonyx jubatus
Male
One year old
See pages 28-38, 42 and 43

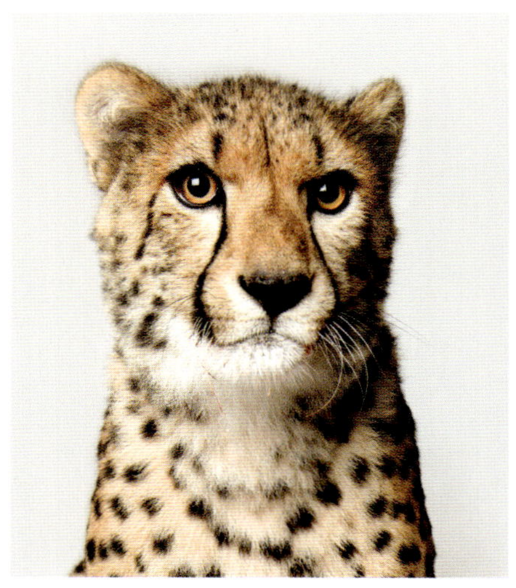

RAMESE

Cheetah
Acinonyx jubatus
Male
One year old
See pages 31, 34, 35, 39, 40 and 41

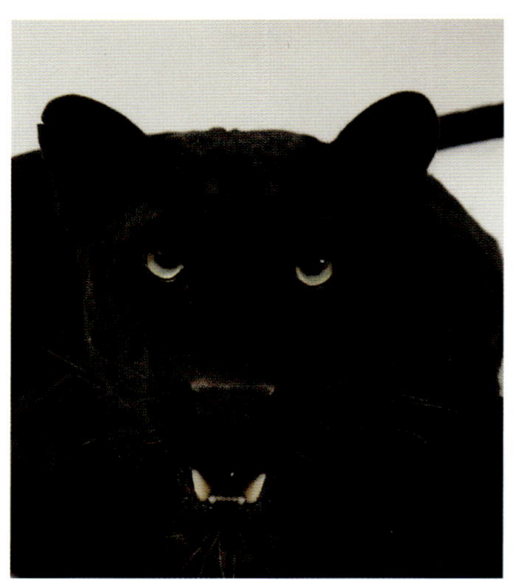

BIJA

Black leopard
Panthera pardus
Female
Two years old
See pages 22, 26 and 27

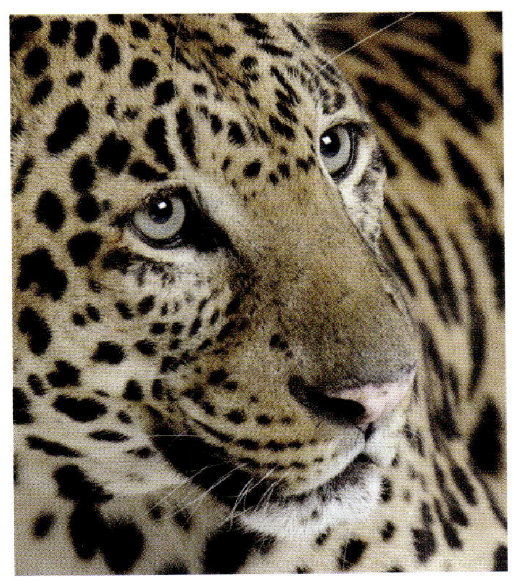

JAPA

Leopard
Panthera pardus
Male
Three years old
See pages 17–20 and 24

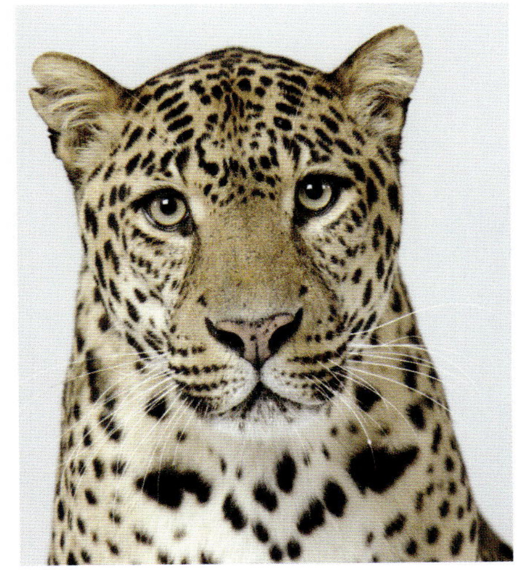

CHANCE

Leopard
Panthera pardus
Male
Three years old
See pages 12, 21, 23 and 25

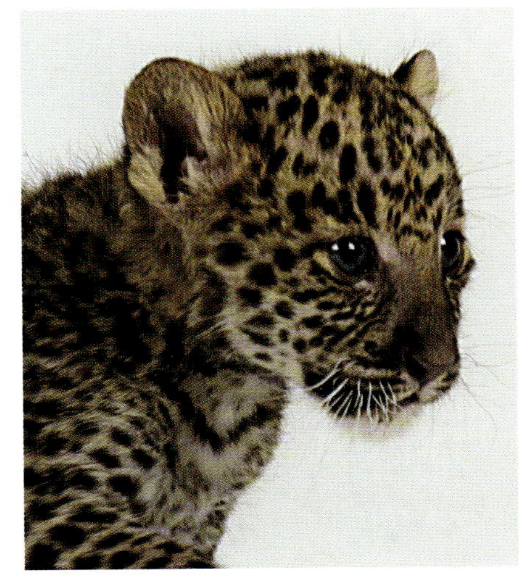

CHANT

Leopard
Panthera pardus
Male
Six weeks old
See pages 14 and 15

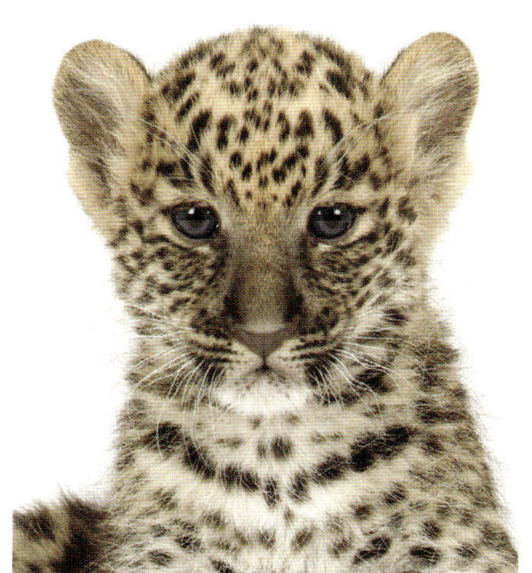

SLOKA

Leopard
Panthera pardus
Male
Six weeks old
See pages 14 and 16

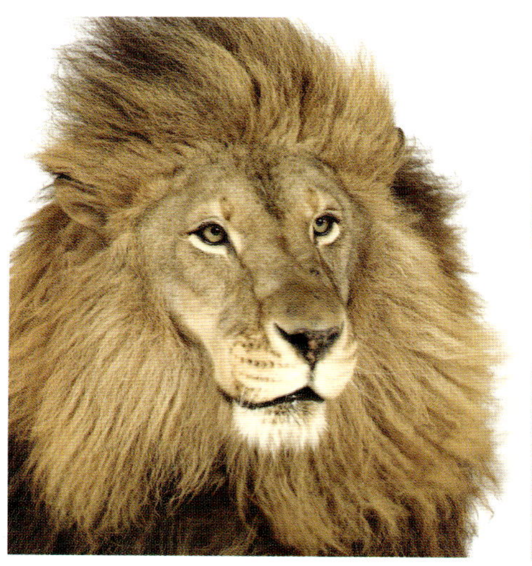

ASLAN

Lion
Leo Panthera
Male
Fourteen years old
See pages 44 and 47–49

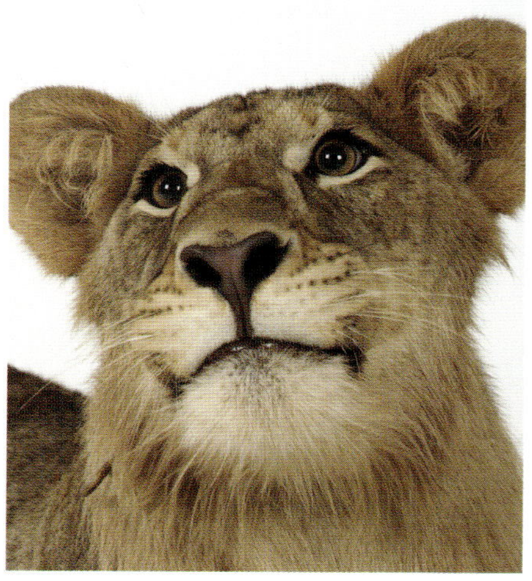

JAGA

Lion
Leo Panthera
Male
Ten months old
See pages 50–51

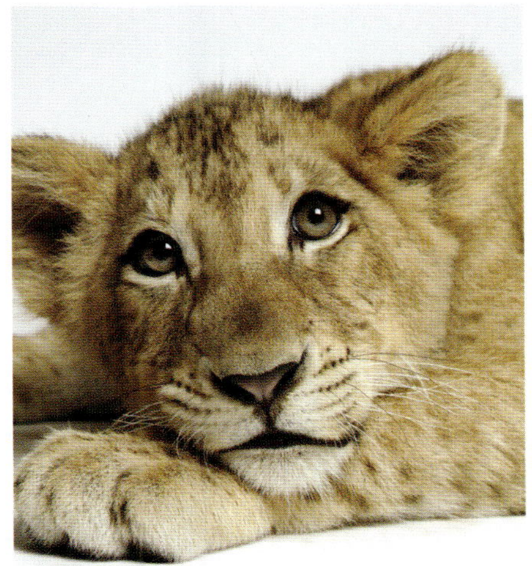

NGALA

Lion
Leo Panthera
Male
Four months old
See pages 46

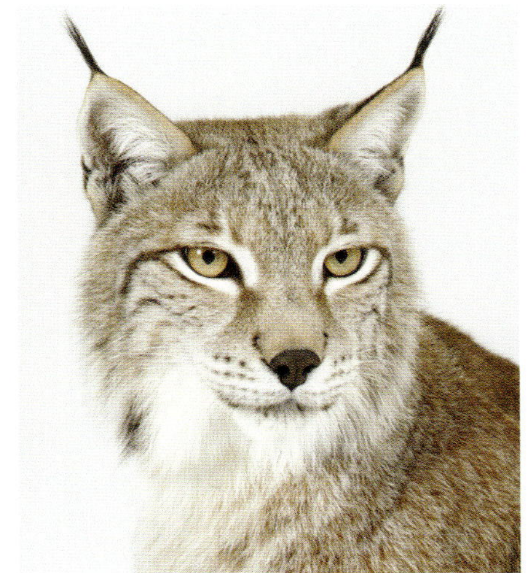

PARVATI

Lynx
Lynx lynx wrangeli
Female
Three years old
See pages 52–61

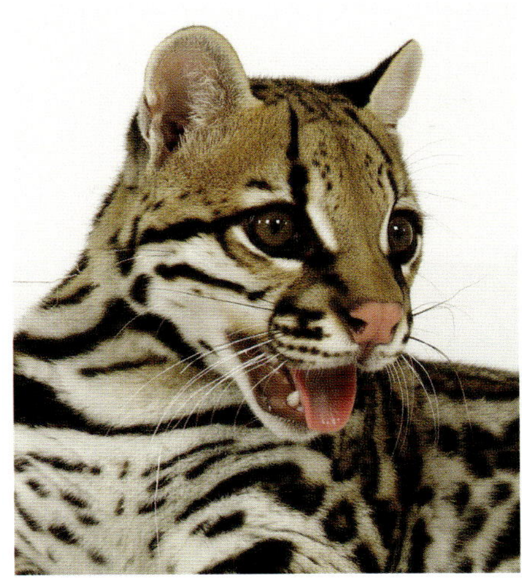

TOLTEC

Ocelot
Leopardus pardalis
Male
Seven months old
See pages 62–71

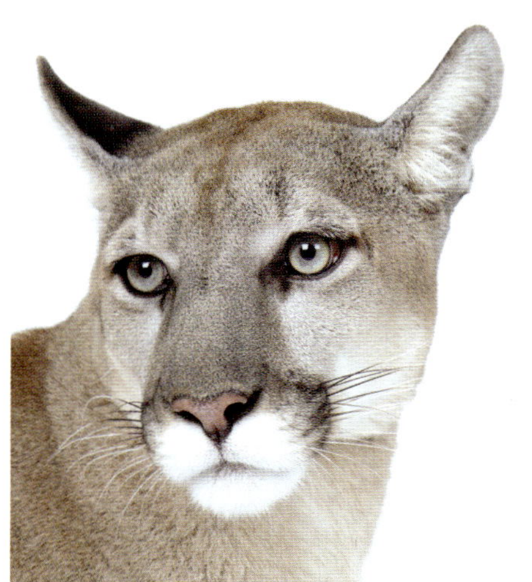

SEQUIA

Panther
Puma concolor coryi
Male
Six years old
See pages 72–81

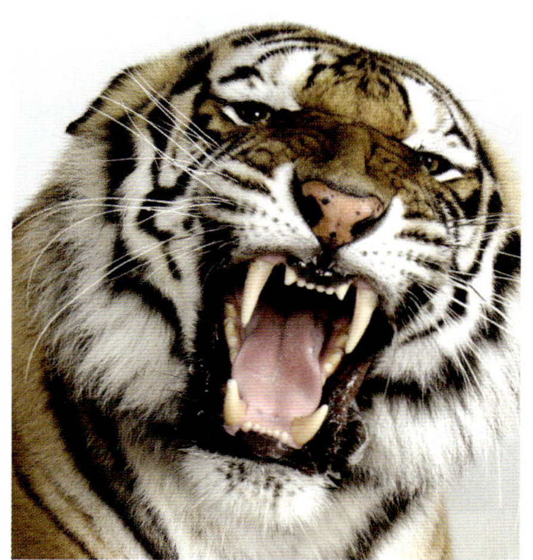

KANGA

Bengal tiger
Panthera tigris
female
Eight years old
See pages 82 and 94

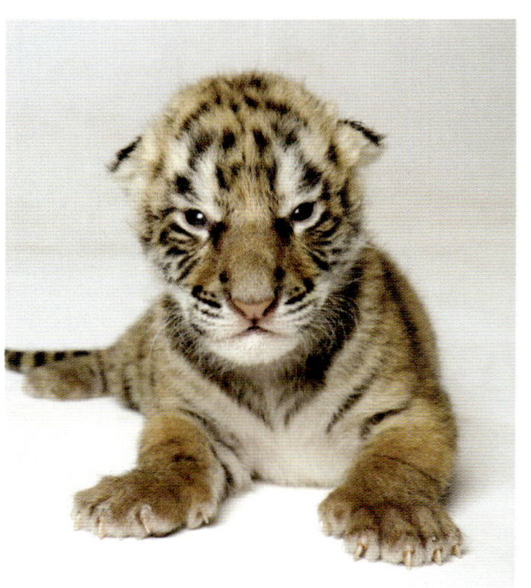

GOVINDA

Bengal tiger
Panthera tigris
Male
Three weeks old
See page 84

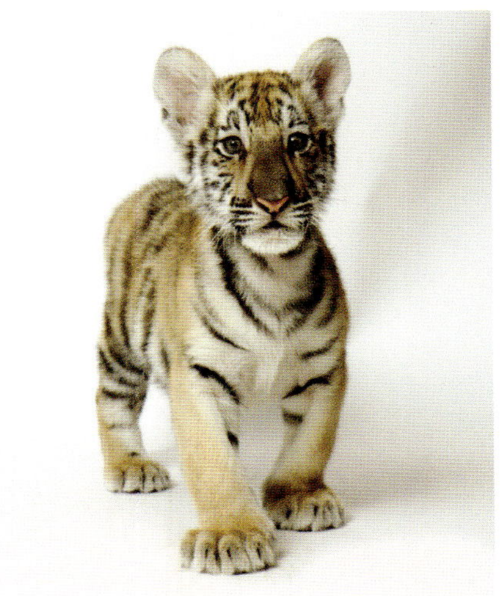

TYRA

Bengal tiger
Panthera tigris
Female
Seven weeks old
See pages 85, 87 and 88

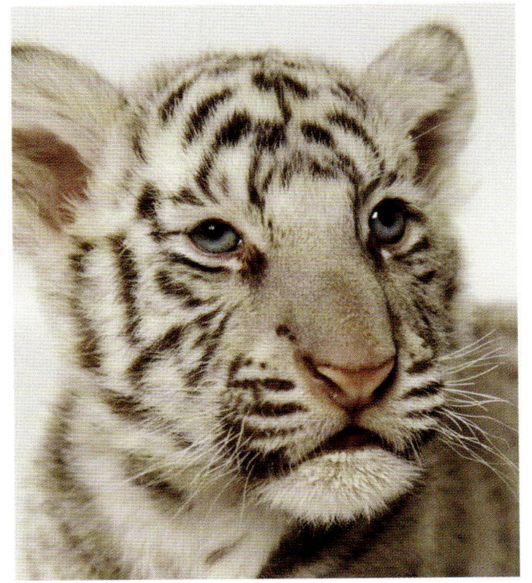

KRISHNA

Royal white tiger
Panthera tigris
Male
Seven weeks old
See pages 86–87

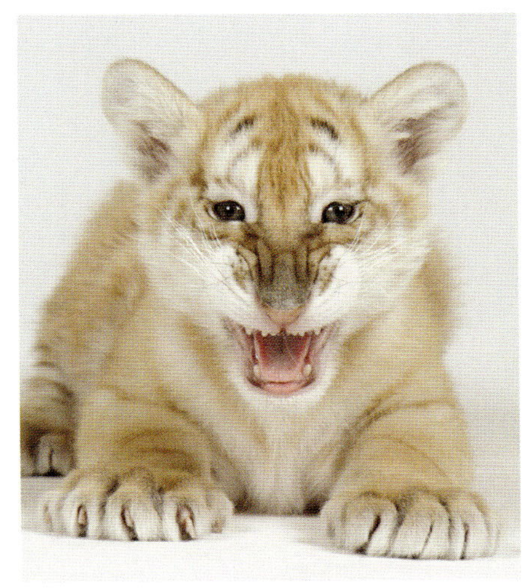

RADHA

Golden tabby tiger
Panthera tigris
female
Two months old
See page 89

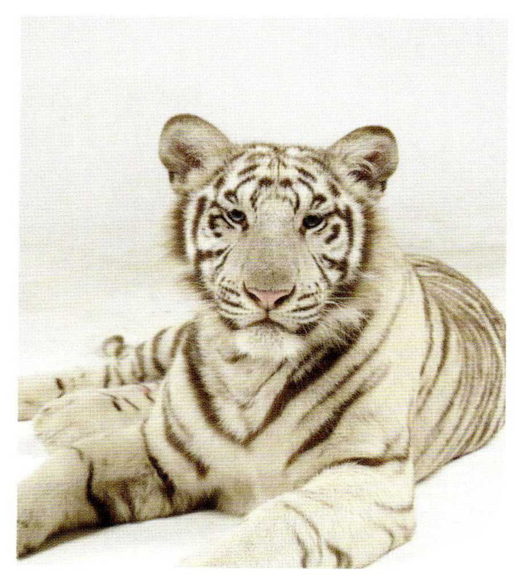

ATMA

Royal white tiger
Panthera tigris
Female
Two years old
See page 90

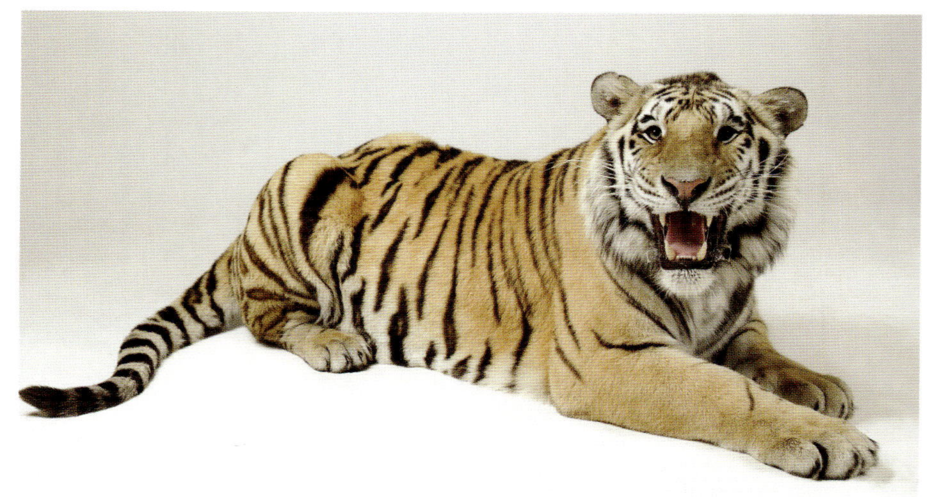

MORTAYE

Bengal tiger
Panthera tigris
Male
Two years old
See pages 92–93, 97 and 99

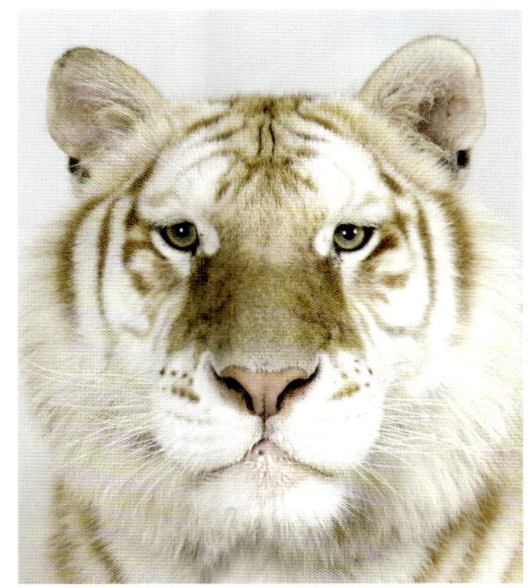

MAHESH

Golden tabby
Panthera tigris
Male
Two years old
See page 95

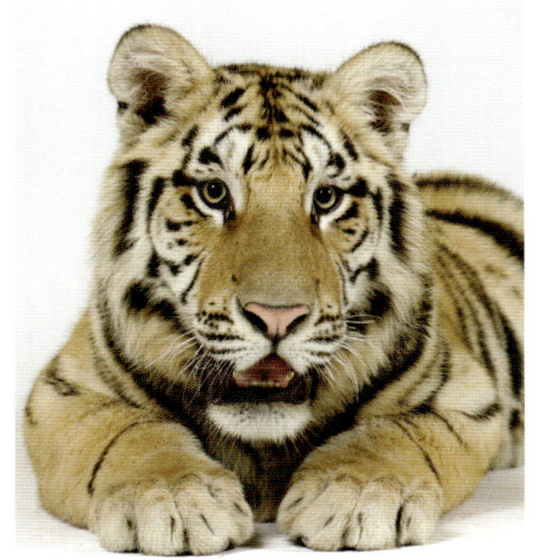

GOPAL

Bengal tiger
Panthera tigris
Male
One year old
See page 91

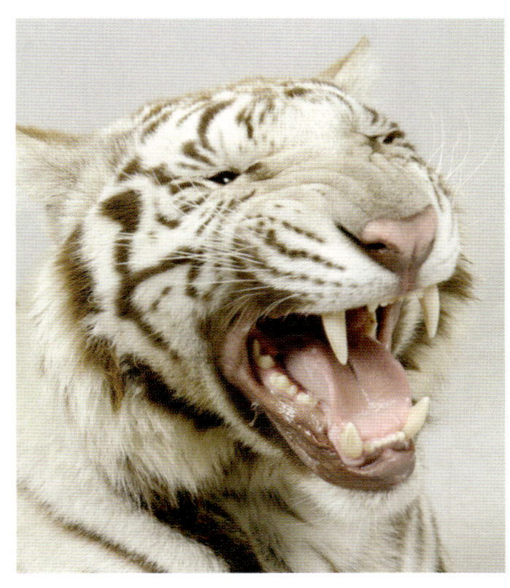

NARYANA

Royal white tiger
Panthera tigris
Male
Three years old
See page 96

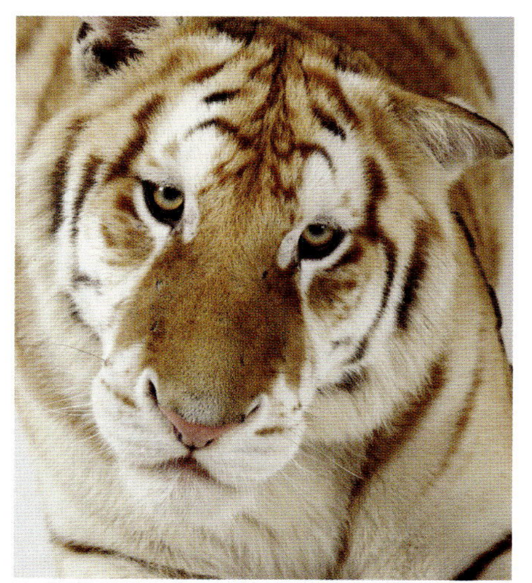

MUHKTAN

Golden tabby tiger
Panthera tigris
Male
Three years old
See page 98

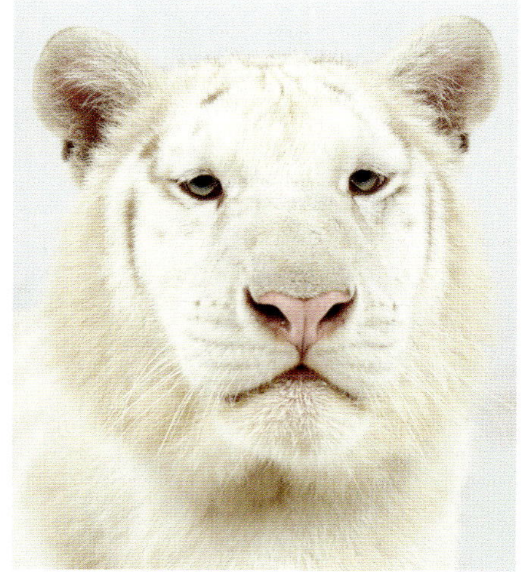

SUNDARI

Snow white tiger
Panthera tigris
Female
Four years old
See page 100

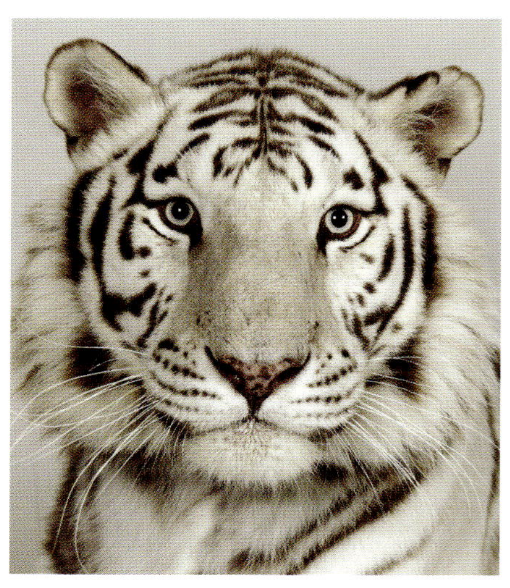

GANGA

Royal white tiger
Panthera tigris
Female
Eight years old
See page 101

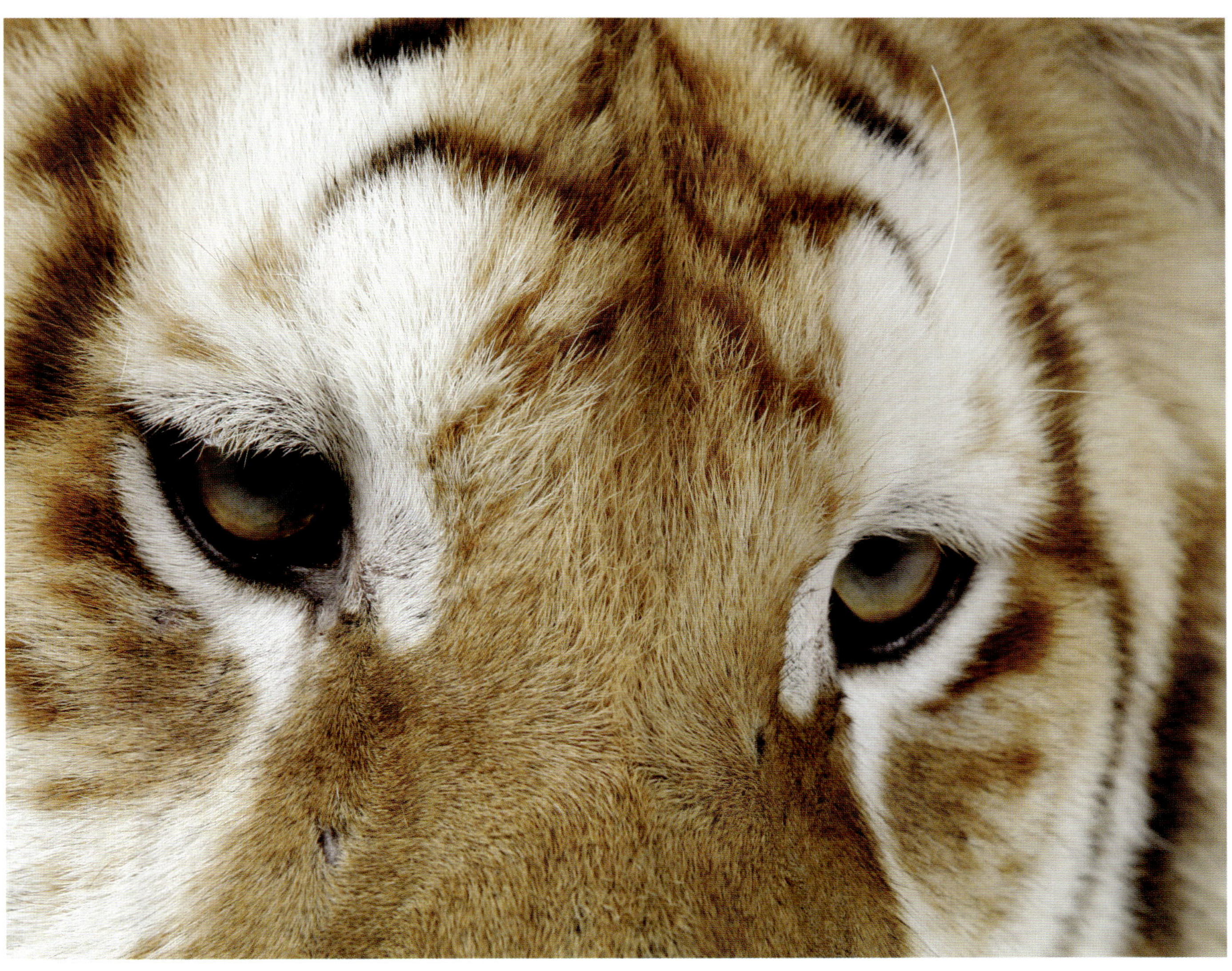

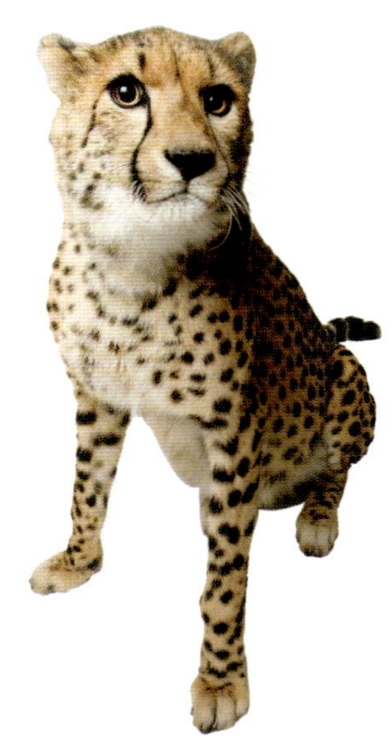

To purchase an image from this book visit:
www.TigerPortraits.com

Ammonite Press
AE Publications Ltd, 166 High Street, Lewes, East Sussex,
BN7 1XU, United Kingdom
Tel: 01273 488005 Fax: 01273 402866
www.ae-publications.com